# Keep Calm And Listen
## The Mirror Britain Won

by James Thornfield

Copyright © 2025. All rights reserved.

The views and opinions expressed in this book are those of the author and do not necessarily reflect the official policy or position of any organization, institution, or government. This book contains critical analysis of public figures, institutions, and policies based on publicly available information, official statistics, and the author's personal observations and analysis.

All statistical data and references cited are from publicly available sources. While every effort has been made to ensure accuracy, readers are encouraged to verify information independently. The author accepts no responsibility for any actions taken based on the content of this book.

This work is intended as social and political commentary.

Any resemblance to actual events or persons, living or dead, is purely coincidental where fictional examples are used for illustrative purposes.

The author writes under a pen name to maintain professional independence and personal privacy.

# Table of Contents

*Introduction* .................................................................... 3

*The Glory Days That Never Were: Football's False Dawn* ... 6

*The Myth of Standing Alone: Britain's Borrowed Victory* . 14

*Heroes and Homeless: The Military Hypocrisy* ................. 21

*Brexit: The Sovereignty Delusion* ....................................... 29

*The NHS: Sacred Cow, Broken System* ............................... 36

*The U.S.A. And The Special Relationship That Isn't* .......... 49

*Class Warfare: The Persistent Elite* ................................... 57

*Weather: The Great Distraction* ......................................... 73

*The Queue Mythology* ......................................................... 83

*The Customer Service Con* ................................................. 93

*Financial Services: The Hollow Crown* ............................ 103

*The Innovation Illusion* ..................................................... 112

*Housing: The Speculation Economy* ................................ 122

*Imperial Nostalgia: The Phantom Empire* ...................... 132

*The "Royal" Mail Scandal: When Institutions Fail* .......... 153

*A Conclusion* ...................................................................... 176

# Introduction

I came to Britain twenty years ago with the reverence that many foreigners hold for this country, admiration for its history, respect for its institutions, and genuine affection for its people. Like millions of others, I believed in the Britain that projects itself to the world: a nation of quiet competence, democratic wisdom, and understated excellence. I expected to find the country that had given the world Shakespeare and Newton, that had stood alone against fascism, that had built a health service envied globally. What I discovered instead was a country living in the past, sustained by myths that bear little relationship to present reality.

This book is not written from hatred but from frustration, the particular frustration that comes from watching a country systematically deceive itself about its own condition. For two decades, I have observed Britain through the eyes of someone who chose to make it home, who has watched friends struggle with housing they cannot afford, who has seen talented colleagues leave for countries that better reward their skills, who has witnessed the gap between political rhetoric and lived reality grow ever wider. The Britain that exists in the imagination of its politicians and much of its media is not the Britain that actually functions day to day.

The purpose of "Keep Calm And Listen" is deliberately provocative: to hold up a mirror that Britain has been studiously avoiding. To trigger honest conversations that are not hidden behind false politeness. This is not an academic exercise or a measured policy critique, this is an intervention, designed to shock a country out of the comfortable delusions that prevent it from addressing genuine problems. Every chapter in this book examines a cherished British myth and confronts it with uncomfortable evidence. The result is not intended to be balanced or diplomatic. It is intended to be true.

From football mythology that turns sporting failure into domestic violence, to NHS worship that excuses healthcare outcomes that would shame developing nations, to queue culture that celebrates managed decline as civic virtue, Britain has constructed an elaborate system of self-deception. These are not harmless quirks or charming eccentricities. They are psychological barriers that prevent honest assessment of national problems and realistic discussion of potential solutions. When a country convinces itself that its failures are actually virtues, it loses the capacity for the self-correction that healthy societies require.

The evidence presented here comes from official statistics, international comparisons, and documented case studies that reveal the human cost of institutional failure disguised as institutional excellence. This is not opinion masquerading as analysis, this is data that British institutions produce but British culture chooses to ignore. The tragedy is not that these problems exist, but that discussing them honestly has become almost impossible within British political and media discourse. Criticism is dismissed as talking the country down, while celebration of mediocrity is praised as patriotic optimism.

My hope is that readers will emerge from this book angry, not at the messenger, but at the waste of human potential that results from a country's refusal to see itself clearly. Britain possesses enormous advantages: a highly educated population, strong institutions, global connections, and cultural influence that far exceeds its economic weight.

But these advantages are being squandered through nostalgia, complacency, and the peculiar British belief that acknowledging problems somehow makes them worse. The mirror I am holding up reflects not a country beyond hope, but a country that has forgotten how to hope effectively. The first step toward improvement is honest recognition of current reality. This book is that recognition, unfiltered and uncompromising. Whether Britain chooses to look into this mirror is, ultimately, up to Britain itself.

# The Glory Days That Never Were: Football's False Dawn

Let's start with the most sacred myth in British culture: that summer evening in 1966 when England beat West Germany 4-2 at Wembley and won the FIFA World Cup. For nearly sixty years, this single victory has been wielded like a talisman against the harsh reality of consistent mediocrity. But this mythology has created something far more dangerous than sporting disappointment, it has warped national psychology and turned football into a proxy for British worth, with consequences that reach into homes, politics, and the nation's ability to confront uncomfortable truths.

England did win the World Cup in 1966. This is not in dispute. What deserves scrutiny is how one tournament victory became the foundation for decades of delusional thinking that now manifests in domestic violence when reality intrudes and dangerous nationalism when modest success feeds existing delusions of grandeur.

The facts about England's subsequent performance are uncomfortable but undeniable. According to FIFA World Cup Statistics Database records spanning 1966 to 2024, England has reached exactly one World Cup final since that July afternoon nearly six decades ago. One. In fifty-eight years of subsequent tournaments, they managed to reach one final, which they lost on penalties to Italy in 2021. This is not the record of a footballing superpower. This is the record of a nation living in the past while using that past to avoid confronting present failures.

Consider the contrast with other major footballing countries. Germany has won the World Cup four times since 1966 and reached eight finals. Brazil has won it three times and reached four finals. France has won it twice and reached four finals. Argentina has won it three times and reached six finals. These countries built their success on systematic improvement rather than historical entitlement. They adapted, evolved, and invested in long-term development programs that produced sustained excellence.

England's response to failure has been to invoke 1966 as evidence that success is England's natural inheritance. The "it's coming home" mentality, popularized during Euro 1996 and repeated obsessively at every major tournament since, perfectly encapsulates this delusion. The phrase suggests football somehow belongs to England, that victory is England's birthright rather than something earned through superior preparation, coaching, and tactical sophistication.

But the most disturbing aspect of this mythology is not sporting underachievement, it is the violence that follows England's predictable failures. The correlation between England's football defeats and domestic abuse is documented fact, not speculation. According to 'When England Lose, Women Pay' (The Independent, 2021), reports of domestic violence increase by 26% when England loses a major tournament match, rising to 38% when England is eliminated from a tournament entirely. The National Centre for Domestic Violence has recorded consistent spikes during England's penalty shootout defeats in 2004, 2006, and 2012, with emergency calls peaking in the hours following England's exits from major competitions.

This pattern reveals something profoundly disturbing about how football mythology has warped British masculinity. When grown men cannot process their national team's predictable failure to live up to inflated expectations, they take out their frustration on the people closest to them. The "it's coming home" mentality has created a cycle where sporting disappointment becomes personal rage, and rage finds its outlet in violence against women and children. This is not the behaviour of a psychologically healthy nation.

The other side of this dependency is equally troubling. On the rare occasions when England achieves modest success, the response reveals a country so starved of genuine achievement that it mistakes competence for greatness. The aftermath of England's 2018 World Cup semifinal appearance was treated as if they had won the tournament. Streets filled with celebrations, newspapers declared a new golden age, and politicians lined up to claim credit for what was essentially a decent run ended by defeat to Croatia.

This pattern repeated during Euro 2020, when England's march to the final triggered proclamations that football genius had returned to its birthplace. The reality was more prosaic: England had avoided every major footballing power until the final, when Italy exposed their limitations with clinical efficiency. But the preceding weeks had seen an explosion of barely contained nationalism that suggested football success would somehow erase decades of decline across multiple areas of British life.

The "football will make Britain great again" mentality is perhaps the most dangerous aspect of the 1966 mythology. It treats sporting success as a substitute for addressing genuine national problems rather than a pleasant distraction from them. When England performs well, conversations about housing crisis, NHS waiting lists, economic stagnation, and social inequality mysteriously disappear from public discourse. Football becomes a narcotic that temporarily numbs the pain of national decline while preventing any serious attempt at diagnosis or treatment.

This dynamic was starkly evident during the COVID-19 pandemic, when England's Euro 2020 run coincided with some of the worst public health failures in Europe. The government's handling of the crisis had resulted in one of the world's highest death rates, but England's football success dominated headlines while excess mortality statistics were relegated to inside pages. As documented in 'Bread and Circuses: How Sport Distracts from Crisis' (Political Quarterly, 2021), major tournament runs consistently correlate with reduced public attention to governmental failures.

Politicians have learned to exploit this dynamic. Policy announcements are timed around major tournaments, knowing that good England performances will overshadow difficult news. The 2016 Brexit referendum campaign strategically avoided major footballing distractions, while the 2019 general election was carefully scheduled to avoid conflict with tournament qualifiers. Football has become a tool of political manipulation, with the 1966 mythology providing the emotional foundation for this exploitation.

The cycle is predictable and pathetic. England stumbles toward a tournament with appropriately low expectations based on recent evidence. Early success triggers wild optimism completely divorced from actual performance levels. Media coverage becomes increasingly hysterical, with tabloid headlines suggesting that victory would somehow restore British greatness on the world stage. When reality intrudes, usually via penalty shootout or tactical superiority from better-coached opponents, the psychological crash is severe. Domestic violence spikes, depression rates increase among male football fans, and the search for scapegoats begins.

Meanwhile, the structural problems that ensure continued failure remain unaddressed. UEFA Tournament Performance Analysis (UEFA, 2020) reveals that England has won zero European Championships since 1966, reached three finals, and been eliminated in early rounds more often than reaching semifinals. This is not bad luck or cruel fate. This is systematic failure disguised as noble effort.

The mythology prevents honest assessment of England's weaknesses because acknowledging them would require admitting that 1966 was an aberration rather than the natural order. England's youth development system consistently produces players who are technically inferior to their European counterparts. English coaching badges are less demanding than those required in Germany, Spain, or the Netherlands. The domestic league, while commercially successful, has become a showcase for foreign talent rather than a development pathway for English players.

Other countries have adapted to modern football's demands through systematic reform. Germany restructured their entire youth system after failing at Euro 2000, investing in technical coaching and tactical education that produced the 2014 World Cup victory. Spain developed their possession-based approach through systematic implementation at club and international level, winning Euro 2008, World Cup 2010, and Euro 2012. France rebuilt their national setup around athletic excellence and tactical flexibility, winning the 2018 World Cup and reaching the 2022 final.

England's response to failure has been to change managers, blame individual players, or cite historical entitlement as evidence that success is inevitable. The fundamental problems remain unaddressed because the 1966 mythology suggests that English football superiority is natural rather than earned through systematic excellence.

But the real tragedy extends beyond football. The violence that follows England defeats is not separate from the arrogance that follows England success, both represent a nation that has confused sporting performance with national worth. Countries with healthier relationships to football treat victories as pleasant surprises and defeats as disappointing but manageable setbacks. Only in Britain does football carry the psychological weight of imperial nostalgia and post-industrial anxiety.

When football becomes the measure of national value, domestic violence after defeats becomes inevitable. When sporting success is treated as proof of inherent superiority, the dangerous nationalism that follows temporary victory becomes equally predictable. Both responses reveal a country that has lost the ability to assess itself honestly, using football results as a substitute for genuine self-knowledge.

To put some numbers behind it, the sad studies of the University of Lancaster suggest a 26% increase of domestic violence when the Three Lions play and win, but a shocking 38% increase in domestic violence when the English team loses (World Cup football is a risk factor for domestic violence, Lancaster University, 2014).

The cost of this delusion is measured not just in tournament failures but in the violence unleashed when those failures occur, and in the toxic nationalism that emerges when modest success feeds existing delusions of grandeur. The Premier League's commercial success has actually made the problem worse, creating the illusion of English football's health while systematically undermining the national team's prospects through reduced opportunities for domestic players.

As detailed in 'The England Managers' (The Telegraph, 2022), this attitude has infected every level of English football, from grassroots coaching to international strategy. The assumption that England deserves success based on historical precedent rather than current merit has created a feedback loop of mediocrity where every decent performance gets hailed as evidence that England is "back," while every failure gets excused as cruel fate.

The tragedy is that England has the resources to build a genuinely competitive football program. The Premier League generates enormous wealth. The country has excellent facilities and passionate support. What it lacks is the honesty to admit that past glory guarantees nothing and that success in modern football requires systematic excellence rather than historical entitlement or mythical birthright.

Until England stops living in 1966, the cycle will continue. Inflated expectations based on ancient history will lead to predictable failure. That failure will trigger violence in homes across the country as men unable to process sporting disappointment lash out at those closest to them. The rare occasions of modest success will trigger dangerous nationalism that treats football victory as proof of broader national superiority, temporarily masking genuine problems while preventing serious reform.

The false dawn of 1966 has become a permanent darkness, blinding England to the reality that football success must be built rather than inherited, and that using sporting results as a measure of national worth corrupts both sport and nation. After nearly sixty years of evidence, perhaps it's time to accept that one good summer does not make a footballing nation, that living in the past guarantees failure in the present, and that the violence and arrogance this mythology produces shame a country that once understood the difference between sporting achievement and national character.

The World Cup is not "coming home" because it was never England's by right. It goes to countries that earn it through superior preparation, coaching, and tactical understanding. Everything else is just mythology dressed up as sporting analysis, with consequences far more serious than missing penalty kicks.

# The Myth of Standing Alone: Britain's Borrowed Victory

The second pillar of British delusion rests on an even more audacious lie than football mythology: the belief that Britain won the Second World War through plucky determination and moral superiority. This narrative, repeated in countless films, books, and political speeches, presents Britain as the heroic nation that stood alone against Nazi tyranny and emerged victorious through Churchill's leadership and the Blitz spirit. The reality is that Britain came within weeks of total collapse in 1940 and survived only through massive American financial support and Soviet sacrifice on an unimaginable scale.

Let's be brutally clear about what actually happened. By June 1940, Britain was effectively bankrupt, militarily defeated, and facing imminent invasion. The British Expeditionary Force had been humiliated at Dunkirk, losing virtually all its equipment. The Royal Navy, while still powerful, could not protect British shipping from German U-boats. Most critically, Britain lacked the industrial capacity and financial resources to continue fighting without external assistance. According to 'The Lend-Lease Program' (US National Archives, 1941-1945), American aid began flowing to Britain months before Pearl Harbor brought the United States into the war, and without this support, British resistance would have collapsed by early 1941.

The myth of "standing alone" ignores the inconvenient fact that Britain was never alone. The Empire provided crucial resources, manpower, and strategic depth. India alone contributed 2.5 million troops to the war effort, while Canada, Australia, and South Africa provided essential industrial support and military personnel. More importantly, American Lend-Lease aid, totalling

$31.4 billion to Britain by 1945 (equivalent to approximately $450 billion today), kept Britain supplied with everything from food to fighter aircraft. As documented in 'Britain's War Machine' (Imperial War Museum, 2019), roughly 60% of Britain's war material came from American production by 1943.

The numbers expose the scale of British dependence on foreign support. Between 1940 and 1945, the United States provided Britain with 17.5 million tons of supplies, including 427,284 trucks, 13,303 combat vehicles, 35,170 motorcycles, and 1.9 million small arms. Without American food shipments, Britain would have faced mass starvation by 1942. Without American fuel, the Royal Air Force would have been grounded. Without American steel and machinery, British war production would have ceased entirely.

But American aid was only part of the story. The decisive factor in Germany's defeat was the Eastern Front, where the Soviet Union absorbed the overwhelming majority of German military effort. Soviet casualties alone numbered approximately 27 million, according to Russian State Archives data from 1945. To put this in perspective, British military and civilian deaths combined totalled roughly 450,000. The Soviets lost sixty times more people than Britain while destroying the bulk of Germany's army, air force, and industrial capacity.

The Battle of Stalingrad, not the Battle of Britain, marked the turning point of the war. By the time British and American forces opened the second front in Normandy in June 1944, German defeat was already assured. The Wehrmacht had been systematically destroyed on the Eastern Front, with over 80% of German military casualties occurring in fighting against Soviet forces. As detailed in 'How Close to Defeat?' (BBC History, 2020), German strategic reserves had been committed to stemming Soviet advances, leaving minimal forces to defend Western Europe.

Winston Churchill himself understood Britain's dependence on allies, despite his post-war mythmaking. His wartime correspondence reveals desperate pleas for American assistance and acknowledgment that Britain could not survive without Soviet success against Germany. In private communications documented in 'The Second World War' by Winston Churchill (Cassell, 1948-1953), Churchill repeatedly expressed fears that Britain would be forced to negotiate peace with Germany if American aid was insufficient or if the Soviet Union collapsed.

The myth becomes even more absurd when examining Britain's strategic position in 1940. The country had no realistic plan for defeating Germany beyond hoping that economic blockade would eventually force German surrender. British military planning documents from the period, now declassified, reveal that the Chiefs of Staff considered German victory probable and recommended negotiating peace terms that would preserve the Empire while accepting German dominance in Europe.

Operation Sea Lion, Germany's planned invasion of Britain, was called off not because of British defensive preparations but because Hitler decided to attack the Soviet Union instead. German naval and military records make clear that invasion plans were shelved due to strategic priorities on the Eastern Front, not British resistance capabilities. The Royal Navy's ability to prevent invasion was theoretical rather than tested, as Germany never seriously attempted large-scale amphibious operations against British shores.

The Battle of Britain itself, while tactically significant, was strategically irrelevant to the war's outcome. German air superiority over Britain would not have guaranteed invasion success, and German defeat in the air battle did not prevent Germany from conquering most of Europe. The decisive battles were fought thousands of miles from British shores, in the vastness of Russia where German armies were systematically destroyed by Soviet forces operating with American equipment and supplies.

British industrial production during the war was dwarfed by American and Soviet output. At its peak in 1943, British aircraft production reached 26,000 units annually, compared to American production of 96,000 units the same year. British tank production peaked at 5,000 units in 1942, while the Soviet Union produced over 24,000 tanks that year despite having lost significant industrial territory to German occupation. Britain was a junior partner in the alliance that defeated Germany, contributing courage and determination but lacking the industrial might necessary for victory.

The post-war narrative conveniently ignores how close Britain came to seeking negotiated peace. In May 1940, the War Cabinet seriously considered peace overtures through Mussolini, with Foreign Secretary Lord Halifax arguing that Britain should explore terms while still possessing some bargaining power. Churchill's refusal to negotiate was based on hope for American intervention rather than confidence in British capabilities. As documented in cabinet minutes now available in the National Archives, Britain's decision to continue fighting was contingent on American promises of support that had not yet materialized.

Even more embarrassing is the reality of British military performance when facing German forces without massive numerical superiority. Every major British offensive in North Africa required multiple attempts before achieving success, and only after receiving substantial American equipment and reinforcements. The invasion of Italy bogged down against determined German resistance despite overwhelming Allied advantages in men, material, and air support. British forces consistently required American support to achieve objectives that German forces accomplished with inferior resources.

The myth of British victory becomes particularly grotesque when considering the post-war settlement. Britain emerged from the war effectively as an American client state, dependent on continued American financial support to avoid economic collapse. The Anglo-American loan of 1946, totalling $3.75 billion, was necessary to prevent British bankruptcy. The Suez Crisis of 1956 demonstrated conclusively that Britain could no longer act as an independent great power, with American financial pressure forcing humiliating withdrawal from military operations.

Yet the mythology persists, poisoning British strategic thinking for decades. The belief that Britain won the war through superior character and determination has justified disastrous military interventions from Suez to Iraq, based on the assumption that British forces possess some mystical superiority over foreign opponents. The reality is that British military success in World War Two was entirely dependent on fighting as part of a coalition where other allies provided the decisive military and industrial contributions.

This delusion has infected British politics at the highest levels. Brexit was sold partly on the notion that Britain had defeated Germany before and could do so again economically, ignoring the inconvenient fact that Britain never defeated Germany militarily without massive foreign assistance. The "we stood alone" mythology provided emotional foundation for the belief that Britain could thrive in isolation from European partners, just as it had allegedly thrived in isolation from European allies during the war.

The cost of this mythology extends beyond historical accuracy. It has created a generation of British politicians and citizens who fundamentally misunderstand Britain's place in the world and its dependence on allies for security and prosperity. The belief that Britain won the war through superior national character has justified decades of underinvestment in defence capabilities, based on the assumption that British pluck will triumph over foreign efficiency when circumstances require.

Modern British military capabilities reflect this complacency. The Royal Navy operates fewer major surface vessels than Italy. The Royal Air Force fields fewer combat aircraft than Poland. The British Army is smaller than it has been at any time since the Napoleonic Wars. Yet the mythology of wartime victory continues to support the illusion that Britain remains a major military power capable of independent action on the world stage.

The tragedy is that Britain's actual contribution to Allied victory was significant and honourable. British resistance in 1940 provided a base for eventual Allied operations. British intelligence services made crucial contributions to the war effort. British scientists and engineers developed radar, code-breaking capabilities, and other technologies that aided Allied success. The Royal Navy's protection of Atlantic shipping lanes was essential to maintaining the flow of supplies that sustained Soviet resistance.

But these genuine achievements have been inflated into a mythology that obscures the decisive contributions of allies and creates dangerous illusions about British capabilities. The result is a country that cannot assess its current position honestly because it remains intoxicated by a distorted version of its past, mistaking borrowed victory for indigenous strength, and allied success for national triumph.

Until Britain acknowledges that its survival and eventual victory in World War Two depended entirely on American resources and Soviet sacrifice, it will continue to make strategic errors based on historical fantasies rather than contemporary realities. The myth of standing alone has become a permanent delusion, preventing honest assessment of British strengths and weaknesses while justifying policies based on nostalgic fiction rather than practical necessity.

# Heroes and Homeless: The Military Hypocrisy

British military mythology presents a nation that honours its armed forces above all else, celebrating their sacrifice while supporting them through thick and thin. The reality reveals a breathtaking hypocrisy: Britain eagerly sends young men and women to fight unnecessary wars based on dubious intelligence and political expediency, then abandons them to homelessness, poverty, and charity when they return damaged by experiences their country demanded they endure.

The statistics are damning and undeniable. According to 'State of Veterans' (Royal British Legion, 2023), approximately 13,000 military veterans are homeless across the United Kingdom, representing roughly 8% of the total homeless population. These are people who served their country in conflicts from Northern Ireland to Afghanistan, who followed orders without question and fulfilled duties that politicians deemed essential for national security. Their reward for this service is sleeping rough on the streets of the cities they once protected.

Crisis UK's 2024 homeless veterans study reveals that former military personnel are twice as likely to experience homelessness as civilians, with rates particularly high among those who served in Iraq and Afghanistan. The average time between military discharge and first homelessness episode is just eighteen months, suggesting that the transition support system is not merely inadequate but virtually non-existent. These veterans cite a combination of post-traumatic stress disorder, difficulty finding employment, family breakdown, and substance abuse as contributing factors to their homelessness, all predictable consequences of military service that successive governments have failed to address systematically.

Yet British defence spending continues to prioritize expensive equipment over veteran care. Ministry of Defence Budget Reports from 2020-2024 show that while procurement spending has increased by 15% over the period, veteran support services have seen budget cuts in real terms. The MOD spent £48.8 billion in 2023, with the vast majority allocated to purchasing weapons systems that will likely prove as useless as the equipment deployed in Iraq and Afghanistan. Meanwhile, veteran housing support received £127 million, less than the cost of a single Type 26 frigate.

The pattern is consistent and morally reprehensible. Britain commits military forces to conflicts that serve no clear national interest, sustains those conflicts for years beyond any reasonable strategic objective, then cuts support for the people damaged by these experiences. The wars themselves are typically justified by intelligence that later proves fabricated, strategic arguments that prove hollow, or humanitarian concerns that prove selective. The human cost is borne by working-class families who provide the military's personnel, while the political and economic benefits accrue to defence contractors and politicians seeking to project strength.

Iraq provides the most egregious example of this pattern. The Chilcot Report (2016) documented in exhaustive detail how Britain committed military forces to an invasion based on intelligence that senior officials knew was unreliable, in pursuit of strategic objectives that were never clearly defined, using military planning that was demonstrably inadequate. The result was 179 British military deaths, hundreds more wounded, and thousands of Iraqi civilian casualties. The strategic outcome was the creation of ISIS and Iranian dominance over Iraq, precisely the opposite of stated British objectives.

But the human cost extends far beyond battlefield casualties. Veterans of the Iraq conflict report PTSD rates of 13%, compared to 3% in the general population. Suicide rates among Iraq veterans are 50% higher than age-matched civilians. Divorce rates are twice the national average. Unemployment among recently discharged Iraq veterans runs at 15%, compared to 4% nationally. These are the predictable consequences of deploying people to fight an unnecessary war in pursuit of objectives that were never achievable.

Afghanistan presents an even starker example of political failure and human waste. Britain maintained military forces in Afghanistan for twenty years, from 2001 to 2021, at a cost of 457 British lives and approximately £37 billion in direct military spending. The stated objective was to deny Afghanistan as a base for international terrorism and to build a stable, democratic government capable of maintaining security independently.

The result was complete failure on every measure. The Taliban returned to power in August 2021 with minimal resistance from Afghan forces that Britain had spent twenty years training and equipping. Afghanistan remains a potential base for international terrorism, now under the control of a movement that has closer ties to international jihadist networks than the Taliban of 2001. Women's rights, which British politicians frequently cited as justification for continued military presence, have been eliminated entirely under renewed Taliban rule.

Yet the political establishment treats this failure as somehow inevitable rather than the predictable result of strategic incompetence and political dishonesty. No senior political or military figures have been held accountable for twenty years of failure that cost hundreds of British lives and tens of billions of pounds while achieving nothing beyond temporary careers advancement for those who managed the disaster.

The veterans of these failed campaigns return to a society that celebrates their sacrifice in abstract terms while providing minimal concrete support. The contrast between public rhetoric and actual policy is staggering. Politicians compete to demonstrate their support for military personnel during ceremonial occasions, wearing poppy pins and attending commemorative events, while voting for budgets that cut veteran services and reduce support for military families.

This hypocrisy extends to the charitable sector that has essentially replaced government responsibility for veteran welfare. The Royal British Legion, Help for Heroes, Combat Stress, and dozens of smaller charities raise hundreds of millions of pounds annually to provide services that should be governmental responsibilities. Citizens are encouraged to donate to veteran charities as a patriotic duty, essentially paying twice for military operations, first through taxes that fund the wars, then through voluntary contributions that support the veterans those wars produce.

The reliance on charity reveals the fundamentally dishonest nature of British military policy. If wars are truly necessary for national security, then supporting the veterans of those wars should be a non-negotiable governmental responsibility funded through taxation rather than voluntary donation. The fact that veteran support depends on charitable fundraising suggests that either the wars are unnecessary or the government refuses to accept the full cost of military operations.

Foreign conflicts continue to be justified through emotional appeals to supporting troops, while actual support for those troops remains inadequate and dependent on charity. This circular logic protects political decision-makers from accountability while ensuring continued public support for military operations that serve no clear national interest. Questioning the wisdom of military intervention becomes equivalent to attacking the troops, while supporting the troops becomes synonymous with supporting whatever military intervention politicians happen to Favor.

The geographic distribution of military recruitment reveals another layer of hypocrisy. According to MOD demographic data, military personnel are disproportionately recruited from economically disadvantaged areas of Scotland, Northern England, and Wales. The children of politicians, senior civil servants, and defence contractors are notably absent from military ranks, despite their families' enthusiasm for military intervention. The people who decide to go to war are not the people who fight those wars, and their children will not bear the consequences of strategic failure.

This class dimension of military service makes the inadequate veteran support particularly offensive. Working-class families provide the personnel for military operations that serve elite political and economic interests, then watch their children return damaged by experiences that the political class considers necessary but would never accept for their own families. The charitable model of veteran support ensures that these same working-class communities must fund the care of veterans through voluntary donations while defence contractors profit from ongoing military operations.

The psychological impact of inadequate veteran support extends beyond individual suffering to broader military effectiveness. Current military personnel observe how veterans are treated and adjust their expectations accordingly. Knowledge that military service leads to homelessness, unemployment, and dependence on charity reduces military recruitment and retention, forcing the MOD to lower standards and offer increasingly generous financial incentives to maintain force levels.

The result is a military that struggles to attract quality personnel despite offering competitive wages and benefits, because potential recruits understand that the social contract between military and society has been broken. They are expected to risk their lives for political objectives they may not understand or support, in the knowledge that inadequate support awaits them if they survive but return damaged by the experience.

Modern British military interventions share common characteristics that should make their failure predictable. They are typically justified by intelligence that proves unreliable, pursue objectives that are never clearly defined, rely on local allies who prove unreliable or corrupt, and continue long beyond any reasonable prospect of success. Yet politicians continue to authorize these operations because the political cost of military failure is transferred to veterans rather than decision-makers.

The contrast with countries that maintain more honest relationships between military service and political decision-making is instructive. Germany's constitutional restrictions on foreign military deployment reflect historical understanding of how easily military intervention can be justified by dubious reasoning and pursued beyond reasonable limits. Switzerland's militia system ensures that military service is distributed across social classes rather than concentrated among the economically disadvantaged.

Britain's military culture, by contrast, encourages interventionism through a combination of historical mythology and social inequality that insulates decision-makers from the consequences of their choices. The result is a country that engages in military operations more frequently than any comparable European nation while providing worse support for military veterans than most developed countries.

The ultimate cost of this hypocrisy is measured not just in individual suffering but in the corruption of democratic decision-making about war and peace. When veteran support is inadequate and dependent on charity, the full cost of military operations is hidden from public view. Citizens can support military intervention while remaining ignorant of its human consequences, because those consequences are displaced to charitable organizations rather than governmental budgets.

Until Britain accepts full governmental responsibility for veteran welfare, military decision-making will remain distorted by the artificial separation between the cost of military operations and the cost of supporting military personnel. Politicians will continue to authorize unnecessary wars because they bear no personal responsibility for the veterans those wars produce, while citizens will continue to support military intervention because its human cost is hidden behind charitable fundraising rather than integrated into public policy.

The heroes sleep rough on British streets while the politicians who sent them to war sleep comfortably in their beds, confident that charitable organizations will manage the human wreckage of strategic incompetence.

This is not honour. This is not patriotism. This is moral cowardice disguised as military virtue, and it shames a nation that once understood the difference between genuine service and political theatre.

# Brexit: The Sovereignty Delusion

The Brexit referendum of 2016 represents the culmination of British delusion, a moment when decades of mythology about standing alone and inherent superiority crystallized into the most catastrophic peacetime decision in modern British history. Sold as "taking back control," Brexit has systematically reduced British sovereignty while increasing dependence on forces beyond British influence. The gap between promise and reality reveals a nation so intoxicated by historical fantasy that it chose economic self-harm over honest assessment of its position in the modern world.

The central lie of the Brexit campaign was that European Union membership somehow constrained British sovereignty. This ignored the reality that sovereignty in the modern world is exercised collectively through international institutions or not at all. No country, regardless of size or historical importance, can unilaterally control global trade flows, climate change, international terrorism, or economic forces that transcend national borders. The choice facing Britain was not between sovereignty and subordination, but between sharing sovereignty within European institutions or surrendering it to forces entirely beyond British control.

The results speak for themselves. Brexit Impact Studies from the Office for Budget Responsibility (2022-2024) show that British trade with the EU has declined by 15% since leaving the single market, while trade with the rest of the world has not increased sufficiently to compensate. British exports face tariff and non-tariff barriers that did not exist as EU members, while British importers struggle with customs procedures that add cost and delay to every transaction. The sovereignty gained is the sovereignty to make trade more difficult and expensive for British businesses.

Financial services, supposedly a British strength that would thrive outside EU regulation, have relocated operations to European cities on a massive scale. According to 'The Brexit Effect' (Financial Times, 2023), approximately £1.6 trillion in assets have been transferred from London to EU financial centres since the referendum, with Amsterdam overtaking London as Europe's largest share trading hub. The City of London's dominance was built on serving as the EU's financial capital, a role that cannot survive outside EU membership regardless of British regulatory flexibility.

Manufacturing has suffered even more severely. Trade Statistics Post-Brexit from the ONS (2024) reveal that British manufacturing exports to the EU have declined by 23% since leaving the single market, with automotive and pharmaceutical sectors particularly affected. Japanese and German manufacturers have relocated production facilities to EU countries to maintain access to European markets, taking jobs and investment that Brexit supporters claimed would be protected by leaving the EU.

The sovereignty argument becomes particularly absurd when examining Britain's current position in international negotiations. Outside the EU, Britain negotiates trade agreements as a market of 67 million people rather than 450 million. The result is consistently worse terms than those achieved through EU membership, with trading partners having little incentive to offer concessions to a diminished British market. The US-UK trade negotiations have stalled because America has no interest in meaningful agricultural market access to Britain alone, while comprehensive trade agreements with China remain impossible due to British concerns about human rights and security that carry no weight without EU backing.

Meanwhile, Northern Ireland remains subject to EU regulations through the Northern Ireland Protocol, later renamed the Windsor Framework, because any other arrangement would violate the Good Friday Agreement and trigger renewed sectarian violence. British sovereignty over Northern Ireland is now more constrained than it was as an EU member, with EU law applying directly in British territory without British representation in EU institutions. The Democratic Unionist Party's objections to this arrangement led to the collapse of power-sharing in Northern Ireland for two years, demonstrating how Brexit has weakened rather than strengthened British constitutional integrity.

Scotland presents an even more fundamental challenge to British sovereignty. Scottish Independence Polling from YouGov (2024) consistently shows support for independence running above 50%, driven primarily by opposition to Brexit that Scotland rejected by 62% to 38%. The SNP's argument that Scotland should be independent within the EU has gained credibility as Brexit's economic costs become apparent. British sovereignty may soon extend only to England and Wales, making Brexit the catalyst for the United Kingdom's dissolution rather than its strengthening.

The immigration arguments that drove much of Brexit support have proven equally false. Net immigration to Britain has increased since leaving the EU, reaching record levels in 2022 and 2023. The difference is that EU citizens who contributed to British tax revenues and integrated easily into British society have been replaced by non-EU migrants requiring more extensive support services and facing greater integration challenges. British control over immigration has increased in theoretical terms while the practical results have worsened by every measure Brexit supporters claimed to care about.

Regulatory sovereignty, another key Brexit promise, has proven largely meaningless. British businesses operating internationally must comply with EU regulations regardless of British legal requirements, because the EU market remains Britain's largest trading partner. British pharmaceutical companies must meet EU standards to sell in European markets. British financial services must comply with EU regulations to serve European clients. The result is that British businesses face the cost of dual regulatory compliance without gaining meaningful competitive advantages from British regulatory flexibility.

The European Research Group and other Brexit advocates promised that leaving the EU would allow Britain to pursue a more global trading strategy, reducing dependence on European markets through increased trade with Commonwealth countries and emerging economies. The reality has been the opposite. Trade Statistics Post-Brexit show that the proportion of British trade conducted with EU countries has declined only marginally, while trade with Commonwealth countries has not increased sufficiently to compensate for lost European trade. Geography and economic structure matter more than historical sentiment or political preference.

Perhaps most embarrassingly, Brexit has increased British dependence on EU cooperation in areas where sovereignty matters most. British security services rely on European intelligence sharing to combat terrorism and organized crime, but now operate as junior partners rather than equal participants in European security arrangements. Climate change policy requires European coordination that Britain can influence less effectively outside EU institutions. Even fish, the totemic Brexit issue that symbolized British sovereignty over natural resources, continue to be managed through agreements with EU countries because fish populations do not respect national boundaries.

The Northern Ireland border issue exposed the fundamental incoherence of Brexit sovereignty claims. British politicians simultaneously demanded control over British borders and maintenance of an open border with the EU through Ireland. These objectives are mutually exclusive, but acknowledging this would have required admitting that sovereignty involves trade-offs rather than pure gain. The result was years of negotiation that produced arrangements satisfying nobody while demonstrating British inability to achieve contradictory objectives through political will alone.

European courts continue to influence British law through the European Convention on Human Rights, which predates EU membership and remains binding regardless of Brexit. British politicians who claimed that leaving the EU would restore British legal sovereignty now discover that international law constrains national sovereignty in ways that EU membership actually helped manage. The sovereignty gained from leaving EU institutions is undermined by the necessity of engaging with European institutions through less favourable arrangements.

Trade negotiations with non-EU countries have consistently failed to deliver the benefits Brexit advocates promised. The Australia trade agreement provides minimal economic benefit while potentially damaging British agriculture through increased competition. The India trade negotiations have stalled over visa arrangements that highlight how sovereignty over immigration policy constrains sovereignty over trade policy. The CPTPP membership application demonstrates that even Pacific trade arrangements require surrendering sovereignty over regulatory policy to international bodies less sympathetic to British interests than EU institutions.

The political establishment's response to Brexit's evident failure has been to deny rather than acknowledge the scale of the disaster. Conservative politicians who championed Brexit now blame implementation rather than conception for disappointing results. Labour politicians who opposed Brexit avoid discussing reversal options because they fear electoral consequences of admitting the scale of the mistake. The result is a conspiracy of silence that prevents honest assessment of Brexit's costs while ensuring continued economic and political damage.

Scotland's independence movement has gained momentum precisely because Brexit demonstrated that British political institutions are incapable of honest self-assessment. Scottish voters observe the gap between Brexit promises and results, conclude that British political judgment is fundamentally flawed, and seek independence as protection against future British strategic errors. Brexit's attempt to strengthen British sovereignty has created the conditions for British dissolution.

The cost of Brexit extends beyond immediate economic damage to long-term British credibility in international affairs. European partners who spent decades building cooperative relationships with Britain now view British commitments as unreliable and British political judgment as suspect. American allies question British strategic thinking after watching Brexit's effects on British economic and political stability. The soft power advantages that once compensated for British economic and military decline have been squandered through demonstrable policy failure.

Brexit represents the triumph of mythology over reality, sovereignty claims over sovereignty practice, and historical nostalgia over contemporary analysis. The belief that Britain could thrive in isolation from European partners was based on the same delusional thinking that produced football mythology and war mythology: the assumption that British superiority is inherent rather than earned, and that historical success guarantees future achievement regardless of current circumstances.

The sovereignty delusion continues to prevent honest assessment of Britain's position because acknowledging Brexit's failure would require admitting that decades of British political rhetoric has been based on false premises. Politicians cannot admit that EU membership enhanced rather than constrained British sovereignty without revealing their own role in promoting destructive mythology. The result is a country trapped in a policy framework that demonstrably damages British interests while preventing the political honesty necessary for course correction.

Until Britain acknowledges that sovereignty in the modern world requires cooperation with neighbours and partners rather than isolation from them, the country will continue to make strategic errors based on nostalgic fantasy rather than contemporary reality. Brexit's promise of taking back control has delivered the opposite: a Britain with less control over its economic future, reduced influence in international affairs, and diminished capacity to protect its citizens' interests in a globalized world where unilateral action achieves nothing but self-inflicted damage.

# The NHS: Sacred Cow, Broken System

British reverence for the National Health Service borders on religious devotion, with any criticism treated as heresy against the nation's most sacred institution. Politicians compete to demonstrate their NHS loyalty, citizens applaud healthcare workers like wartime heroes, and the service's founding principles are recited like holy scripture. This mythology has created the most dangerous delusion in modern British politics: the belief that worshipping the NHS concept exempts Britain from honestly examining its catastrophic performance compared to other European healthcare systems.

The facts are uncomfortable but undeniable. NHS Performance Statistics from NHS England (2024) reveal waiting times that would trigger government collapse in any other developed country. The median wait for routine surgery is now 14.2 weeks, with some patients waiting over 65 weeks for procedures that could be completed within days in Germany or France. Cancer treatment, supposedly prioritized above all other care, involves delays that directly contribute to preventable deaths. The NHS Constitution promises that patients will begin cancer treatment within 62 days of referral, but only 64% of patients actually receive treatment within this timeframe.

Emergency care has collapsed entirely by international standards. Accident and Emergency departments regularly operate beyond capacity, with patients waiting over 12 hours for admission to hospital beds that frequently do not exist. According to Department of Health data from 2024, ambulance response times for life-threatening emergencies average 10 minutes and 57 seconds, compared to the 8-minute target. For less urgent cases, patients wait an average of 51 minutes for ambulance response, during which time treatable conditions become life-threatening emergencies.

The European Health System Comparisons study from the OECD (2023) places Britain near the bottom of developed country rankings for healthcare outcomes, accessibility, and efficiency. France, Germany, the Netherlands, and Scandinavian countries consistently deliver better health outcomes with comparable or lower per-capita spending. These countries achieve superior results through mixed public-private systems that combine universal coverage with efficient delivery mechanisms. Britain achieves inferior results through ideological commitment to a delivery model that prioritizes political symbolism over patient care.

Cancer survival rates reveal the human cost of NHS mythology. Five-year survival rates for common cancers lag significantly behind European averages, with Britain ranking 19th out of 23 developed countries for cancer outcomes according to 'The NHS at 75' (British Medical Journal, 2023). Breast cancer survival rates in Britain are 81%, compared to 87% in Germany and 86% in France. Lung cancer survival rates are even worse, with Britain achieving 13% five-year survival compared to 21% in Germany and 17% in France. These differences represent thousands of preventable deaths annually, sacrificed to maintain ideological purity about healthcare delivery.

The waiting time crisis extends far beyond routine procedures to emergency interventions that determine life and death. Cardiac surgery waiting times average 26 weeks, during which patients suffer heart attacks that could have been prevented through timely intervention. Hip and knee replacements, essential for maintaining quality of life among elderly patients, involve waits of over 30 weeks that condemn patients to months of unnecessary pain and immobility. Mental health services, supposedly prioritized by successive governments, involve waits of over 12 weeks for initial assessment and months more for actual treatment.

Yet criticism of NHS performance is treated as political sacrilege rather than legitimate concern for patient welfare. The phrase "our NHS" is deployed to shut down discussion of reform options that might improve patient outcomes through alternative delivery mechanisms. Any suggestion that private sector involvement might improve efficiency or reduce waiting times is dismissed as "privatization" regardless of evidence from European countries that achieve superior results through mixed systems.

This intellectual dishonesty has created a feedback loop where NHS failure generates increased political support for NHS funding without corresponding pressure for NHS reform. Every winter crisis, every scandal about patient neglect, every report of preventable deaths is met with demands for more money rather than better management. Politicians respond with increased NHS budgets that disappear into bureaucratic structures without improving patient care, because the fundamental delivery model remains unchanged regardless of funding levels.

The international comparison is devastating for British complacency. Germany's healthcare system provides universal coverage through a combination of public insurance and private delivery that achieves waiting times measured in days rather than months. Patients receive same-day appointments with specialists, immediate access to diagnostic procedures, and surgery scheduled within weeks of diagnosis. German healthcare spending per capita is marginally higher than British spending, but outcomes are dramatically superior across every measure.

France's healthcare system, ranked first globally by the World Health Organization, combines public funding with private delivery to achieve outcomes that shame British performance. French patients wait an average of 11 days for specialist appointments compared to 14 weeks in Britain. Cancer survival rates exceed British performance by margins that represent thousands of lives saved annually. French healthcare spending is comparable to British spending, but efficiency is far superior because ideology does not prevent practical solutions to delivery problems.

The Netherlands provides universal healthcare through regulated private insurance that achieves waiting times and outcomes that make the NHS look like a developing country health system. Dutch patients receive specialist care within days, complex surgery within weeks, and emergency care that meets response time targets the NHS abandoned years ago. Dutch healthcare spending per capita is lower than British spending, but results are superior because efficiency matters more than political symbolism.

Even the United States, despite its obvious flaws in coverage and affordability, delivers superior outcomes for patients who can access care. American cancer survival rates exceed British performance across all major cancers. American surgical waiting times are measured in days rather than months. American emergency care, while expensive, provides rapid response that British patients can only dream of receiving. The contrast suggests that NHS problems extend beyond funding to fundamental structural failures that money alone cannot address.

The mythology prevents honest discussion of reform options because any deviation from pure public provision is treated as betrayal of NHS founding principles. This ideological rigidity has trapped British healthcare in a delivery model designed for the economic and social conditions of 1948, when medical technology was primitive, demographic patterns were different, and patient expectations were lower. Modern healthcare requires flexibility, efficiency, and responsiveness that the NHS structure cannot provide regardless of funding levels.

Private healthcare in Britain operates as a parallel system that highlights NHS failures while providing escape routes for those wealthy enough to afford alternatives. Private patients receive immediate specialist consultations, rapid diagnostic procedures, and surgery scheduled at their convenience. The same consultants who tell NHS patients to wait months for routine procedures provide identical treatment to private patients within days. This two-tier system undermines NHS universality while protecting political and economic elites from the consequences of NHS failure.

The staff shortage crisis reveals how NHS mythology damages the very healthcare workers it claims to celebrate. Nursing vacancies run at over 40,000 positions nationally, while doctor recruitment struggles to fill positions that offer poor working conditions, inadequate resources, and impossible patient loads. Experienced healthcare professionals emigrate to countries that offer better working conditions and superior patient care, while British medical schools train doctors who frequently pursue careers abroad rather than accepting NHS employment conditions.

The result is a healthcare system increasingly dependent on foreign-trained staff who view NHS employment as temporary rather than permanent career choices. British healthcare depends on doctors and nurses trained at foreign expense who return to their home countries once they accumulate sufficient British work experience. This brain drain from developing countries subsidizes British healthcare while ensuring continued NHS staffing instability.

Administrative bloat consumes resources that could fund patient care, with NHS management structures that would embarrass private corporations forced to justify their efficiency. According to NHS workforce statistics, administrative positions have increased by 40% over the past decade while nursing positions have increased by only 12%. Managers manage other managers in bureaucratic hierarchies that multiply costs while reducing accountability for patient outcomes. The NHS employs more administrators per patient than any comparable healthcare system, yet delivers worse results than countries with leaner management structures.

The COVID-19 pandemic exposed NHS operational failures that decades of increased funding had failed to address. Britain suffered one of the world's highest death rates despite advance warning about pandemic risks and despite NHS claims about emergency preparedness. Ventilator shortages, PPE failures, and testing delays revealed a healthcare system incapable of responding effectively to predictable challenges. The subsequent inquiry recommendations will be ignored, as previous inquiry recommendations have been ignored, because implementing changes would require admitting that NHS mythology prevents practical improvements.

Mental health services provide perhaps the starkest example of NHS failure disguised as NHS virtue. Waiting times for mental health treatment average 18 weeks for initial assessment, with many patients waiting over six months for actual therapy. Suicide rates among patients waiting for mental health treatment exceed rates in comparable countries that provide timely intervention. Yet politicians continue to promise mental health parity with physical health while maintaining delivery systems that guarantee treatment delays incompatible with effective mental health intervention.

The contrast with European mental health services is particularly damning. German patients receive mental health assessment within days and treatment within weeks through systems that integrate public funding with private delivery. French mental health services provide immediate crisis intervention and timely ongoing treatment through mixed systems that prioritize patient outcomes over ideological purity. British patients suffer preventable deterioration while waiting for treatment that arrives too late to be optimally effective.

Emergency care statistics reveal the human cost of NHS mythology most starkly. Ambulance crews spend hours waiting outside hospitals to transfer patients because emergency departments lack capacity to receive them. Heart attack and stroke patients suffer permanent damage while waiting for treatment that could prevent disability if delivered promptly. Elderly patients lie on hospital corridor floors for hours because bed shortages prevent proper accommodation. These scandals generate temporary political attention but no systematic reform because acknowledging the scale of NHS failure would undermine decades of political rhetoric about NHS excellence.

# Real-Life Consequences: When the System Kills

The human cost of NHS mythology becomes starkest when examining individual cases where preventable deaths occur during routine procedures that should carry minimal risk. These cases, while tragic in themselves, reveal systemic failures that the NHS mythology prevents from being honestly addressed.

The case of Susan Evans demonstrates exactly how NHS mythology masks systemic failures that cost lives. Susan Evans, 55, underwent elective gastric bypass surgery at Queen Alexandra Hospital in Portsmouth on July 11, 2023. The surgery went to plan, but she experienced abdominal pain in the early hours of July 13, which was the first day of industrial action by junior doctors. What happened next illustrates precisely the kind of post-operative monitoring failures that occur regularly in overstretched NHS hospitals.

The coroner said there was no specialist weight loss nurse on duty, and Ms Evans was not seen by a senior doctor. Contrary to Queen Alexandra hospital's written policy for gastric bypass patients, Ms Evans was not seen by a member of the specialist bariatric team and was not seen by a senior doctor after reporting pain in order to rule out the possibility of an anastomotic leak. The coroner's findings reveal systematic protocol failures that directly contributed to preventable death.

Ms Evans was discharged but returned to Queen Alexandra Hospital days later by which point she was extremely unwell with abdominal sepsis from an anastomotic leak. Despite appropriate medical care following her re-admission, her condition deteriorated, and she died at Queen Alexandra Hospital on August 12, 2023. It is likely that, if she had been seen by a member of the bariatric team on July 13, 2023, she would have been kept in hospital and would have been operated upon sooner.

The case becomes even more damning when examining the systematic policy failures. The coroner said that under Queen Alexandra's post-operation care guidance, a bariatric specialist nurse, consultant or registrar, was required to carry out a daily review on patients who had weight loss surgery. Neither the written nor informal policy set out above were followed in Ms Evans' case. The failure to follow policy contributed more than minimally to Ms Evans death.

Another case reveals how NHS failures cascade from simple diagnostic errors into preventable deaths. Thomas Gibson, 40, died on the morning his partner gave birth to their daughter after NHS doctors failed to correctly interpret a routine ECG scan. Thomas had been seen at Wythenshawe Hospital in Manchester eleven days before his death. When the clinical team were assessing him they did not appreciate that the ECG showed him experiencing complete heart block. Had this been appreciated, Thomas would have been admitted under the care of cardiologists and probably fitted with a pacemaker.

On the day Mr Gibson was due to become a father, his partner Rebecca Moss tried to rouse him as she prepared to go to hospital for an elective Caesarean. "Wake up, it's baby day," she told him but found him "stiff and cold." He was declared dead and she gave birth to their daughter, Harper, the same day. The coroner concluded that Manchester University NHS Foundation Trust's failures directly caused this preventable death.

The ECG that identified a complete heart block was missed by doctors and he was discharged without knowing the dangers of sudden cardiac death. Staff failed to identify that Tom was in serious need of medical attention and no escalation was made that could have saved his life. The expertise which could have saved Tom's life was just one phone call away.

These cases share common characteristics that appear repeatedly in NHS incident reports: staff shortages leading to inadequate monitoring, failure to follow established protocols, delayed medical response to deteriorating conditions, and over-reliance on junior staff to make critical decisions. In 2024, there were 713 Prevention of Future Deaths reports issued by coroners, up 25% compared with 2023, highlighting NHS pressures such as long waits, staff shortages and lack of resources.

The human cost extends beyond individual tragedies to broader patterns of preventable harm. Research analysing NHS patient safety incidents found that the most frequent concerns in preventable deaths were failure to keep accurate records or notes (28%), failure in communication or handover (27%) or failure to recognize risk factors or comorbidities (20%). These statistics represent real people suffering preventable complications because NHS systems lack adequate resources and monitoring capabilities to provide safe care.

What makes these cases particularly tragic is that they involve procedures and conditions with excellent outcomes when properly managed. Susan Evans's gastric bypass surgery and Thomas Gibson's heart condition were both entirely treatable with appropriate care and monitoring. The deaths that occurred represent not medical complexity but NHS system failure disguised as unavoidable tragedy.

But NHS mythology prevents honest discussion of these systemic failures because acknowledging them would require admitting that the current delivery model cannot provide safe care regardless of political rhetoric about NHS excellence. The coroner remarked that this inquest was not the first time in recent years that he had heard an inquest involving a young patient who tragically died following sudden cardiac arrest from this hospital where similar issues had arisen.

Instead, each preventable death is treated as an isolated incident, each coroner's Prevention of Future Deaths report is filed away, and each family's grief becomes a private tragedy rather than public accountability for systemic failure. In Wales alone, coroners issued prevention of future deaths reports regarding NHS Wales bodies in relation to 41 deaths since January 2023, with 27 reports issued to Betsi Cadwaladr University Health Board citing "an historic lack of learning within the organisation and poor preparation for inquests."

The contrast with healthcare systems that achieve superior outcomes through mixed delivery models becomes particularly stark when examining these individual cases. In Germany or France, the post-operative monitoring that failed Susan Evans and the diagnostic protocols that failed Thomas Gibson would be provided through adequately staffed systems with clear protocols and rapid response capabilities.

The scale of preventable deaths within the NHS is documented through systematic analysis that reveals patterns the mythology refuses to acknowledge. A study analysing NHS patient-safety-related deaths found that mismanagement of deterioration of acutely ill patients is involved in a third of patient-safety-related deaths, with specific failures including "failure to act on or recognize deterioration" accounting for 23% of reported incidents. These are not isolated tragedies but systematic failures disguised as individual misfortunes.

The solution requires abandoning NHS mythology in Favor of honest assessment of healthcare delivery options. European countries achieve universal healthcare through various mechanisms that combine public funding with efficient delivery systems. Britain could achieve superior health outcomes through reform models that maintain universal coverage while improving operational efficiency. But such reforms require admitting that the current NHS model fails patients in ways that alternative approaches could address.

Until Britain stops worshipping the NHS concept and starts measuring NHS performance against international standards, British patients will continue to suffer preventable deaths, unnecessary delays, and inferior outcomes compared to patients in countries that prioritize healthcare effectiveness over healthcare ideology. The sacred cow has become a sick cow, but killing it requires political courage that British politicians lack because NHS mythology has become more important than NHS reality.

Until Britain stops treating NHS failure as exceptional rather than predictable, these preventable deaths will continue to occur while being dismissed as isolated incidents rather than symptoms of systemic breakdown. The mythology that prevents honest assessment of NHS performance costs lives that could be saved through healthcare systems designed for patient outcomes rather than political symbolism.

The NHS remains free at the point of use while becoming increasingly unavailable at the point of need. This paradox will continue until British politics develops the maturity to distinguish between healthcare principles and healthcare delivery mechanisms, between universal coverage and operational efficiency, between NHS mythology and patient welfare. The choice is clear: reform the NHS or watch British health outcomes continue to lag behind countries that abandoned ideological purity in Favor of practical effectiveness.

# The U.S.A. And The Special Relationship That Isn't

British politicians speak of the "special relationship" with the United States as if it were a marriage of equals, a unique bond forged in the crucible of two world wars and sustained by shared values and mutual respect. This delusion has become so embedded in British foreign policy thinking that questioning it borders on treason against the national narrative. The reality is that Britain's "special relationship" with America is a one-sided fantasy, a diplomatic fiction that serves American interests while providing Britain with the illusion of influence it lost decades ago.

The evidence of this delusion is overwhelming and humiliating. When Britain needed American support during the Suez Crisis of 1956, President Eisenhower forced British withdrawal through economic pressure that threatened to collapse the pound. When Britain sought to join the European Economic Community, American preferences carried more weight in European capitals than British arguments. When Britain wanted to maintain its nuclear deterrent, it became entirely dependent on American Trident missiles leased under terms that ensure continued American control.

Modern British foreign policy operates as an echo chamber where American initiatives are reflexively supported regardless of British interests. Britain participated in the Iraq invasion based on American intelligence that British officials knew was unreliable, pursuing American strategic objectives that contradicted British regional interests. Britain committed forces to Afghanistan for twenty years in support of American strategic goals that were never clearly defined and ultimately proved unachievable. Britain imposed economic sanctions on Russia that damaged British energy security while American energy exports to Europe increased substantially.

The institutional framework of this relationship reveals its fundamentally unequal nature. According to US Foreign Policy Priorities from the State Department (2024), Britain ranks behind Canada, Mexico, Japan, and South Korea in American strategic considerations. The AUKUS partnership explicitly excluded Britain from the submarine technology transfer that forms its core component, with Australia receiving American nuclear technology that Britain has sought for decades. NATO Contribution Statistics from NATO (2024) show that American military spending exceeds the combined defence budgets of all European NATO members, making European strategic autonomy impossible without American consent.

Trade statistics expose the hollow nature of claims about special economic partnership. US-UK Trade Data from the US Trade Representative (2024) shows that Britain accounts for less than 4% of American international trade, while the United States represents nearly 15% of British international trade. This asymmetry reflects Britain's dependence on American markets rather than American dependence on British commerce. The much-vaunted post-Brexit trade negotiations produced minimal tariff reductions and no meaningful market access improvements, because Britain lacks the economic leverage to demand concessions from a market fifteen times larger than its own.

Financial services, supposedly the jewel of British economic strength, exist at American sufferance rather than through British competence. The City of London's role as a dollar clearing centre depends entirely on American regulatory tolerance, which can be withdrawn without consultation or appeal. When America imposed sanctions on Russian financial institutions, British banks complied immediately despite the damage to British commercial interests, because defying American financial regulations would mean exclusion from dollar markets that British banks cannot survive without.

Intelligence sharing, often cited as proof of special partnership, actually demonstrates British subordination to American priorities. The Five Eyes intelligence alliance places Britain in a subordinate role to American agencies that determine which information is shared and which operations receive support. British intelligence services provide valuable human intelligence assets to American operations while receiving electronic intelligence that serves American rather than British strategic objectives. When Edward Snowden revealed the extent of American surveillance cooperation, British intelligence agencies were exposed as junior partners in American operations rather than independent actors pursuing British interests.

Military cooperation follows the same pattern of dependence disguised as partnership. British forces operate American equipment, follow American tactical doctrines, and serve American strategic objectives while maintaining the fiction of independent decision-making. The British nuclear deterrent requires American permission to operate, American maintenance to function, and American targeting information to achieve strategic effect. British aircraft carriers operate American aircraft under American logistical support, making independent British military action impossible without American consent.

Cultural influence flows overwhelmingly from America to Britain rather than creating mutual exchange. American universities dominate global academic rankings while British institutions struggle to maintain international relevance. American technology companies control digital platforms that shape British political discourse and commercial activity. American entertainment companies determine what British audiences watch, hear, and discuss, while British cultural exports represent niche products in American markets rather than mainstream influences.

The diplomatic reality contradicts every assumption underlying the special relationship mythology. When Britain sought American support for its position on the Falklands, Reagan's administration initially favoured Argentina and provided support only when British military success became apparent. When Britain needed American backing during negotiations with the European Union, Trump's administration openly supported EU positions that disadvantaged British interests. When Britain requested American support for post-Brexit trade arrangements, Biden's administration prioritized Irish-American political concerns over British economic needs.

Recent conflicts have exposed the illusory nature of British strategic autonomy within the American alliance system. The withdrawal from Afghanistan proceeded according to American timetables that ignored British operational requirements and strategic concerns. British forces evacuated Kabul under American command, following American priorities, and accepting American decisions about which Afghan allies would be abandoned to Taliban retaliation. The entire twenty-year commitment achieved no British strategic objectives while serving American interests that were ultimately abandoned when those interests changed.

The contrast with countries that maintain genuinely special relationships with the United States reveals the poverty of British claims. Canada exercises effective veto power over American trade and energy policies affecting North American markets. Mexico receives American immigration and border cooperation that reflects genuine mutual dependence. Japan maintains independent foreign policy positions toward China while receiving American security guarantees that serve Japanese rather than American regional interests. South Korea balances American alliance commitments with independent economic relationships that Washington tolerates because Korean strategic importance requires American accommodation.

Britain receives none of these considerations because it provides nothing that America cannot obtain elsewhere or do without entirely. British military contributions to American operations are welcome but not essential. British intelligence assets are useful but not irreplaceable. British diplomatic support is convenient but not necessary. British economic partnership is profitable for both sides but not indispensable for either. The "special relationship" exists in British minds because Britain needs to believe it matters more than the evidence suggests.

The Brexit referendum result demonstrated how thoroughly British politicians had internalized the special relationship delusion. Leave campaigners promised that departing the European Union would allow Britain to strengthen ties with the Commonwealth and pursue closer cooperation with the United States. Both promises proved hollow because neither the Commonwealth countries nor the United States had any interest in arrangements that would privilege British interests over their own strategic and economic priorities.

Commonwealth nations that were once British colonies now pursue independent foreign policies that frequently conflict with British positions. India maintains close relationships with Russia despite British sanctions. South Africa criticizes British positions on international law and human rights. Australia negotiates defence partnerships with the United States that exclude Britain from significant technology transfers. The Commonwealth provides a forum for symbolic cooperation rather than substantive policy coordination, because its members pursue national interests that diverge from British preferences.

The Biden administration's approach to Britain illustrates how American presidents actually view the relationship when freed from ceremonial obligations. Climate change cooperation proceeds through multilateral frameworks where Britain is one voice among many rather than America's primary partner. Technology regulation develops through American-European dialogues where Britain participates as a supplicant rather than an equal partner. Trade policy advances through American-Asian initiatives where Britain has observer status rather than decision-making authority.

Even ceremonial aspects of the relationship reveal its fundamentally unequal nature. American presidents visit Britain when convenient for American political purposes rather than as recognition of British importance. British prime ministers travel to Washington seeking audiences that American presidents grant or withhold based on domestic political calculations rather than international strategic considerations. The much-photographed meetings between British and American leaders serve British domestic political needs while providing Americans with European validation for policies they would pursue regardless of British opinion.

The institutional memory of World War II cooperation provides emotional foundation for the special relationship mythology, but historical analysis reveals that even wartime cooperation was driven by American strategic calculations rather than sentimental attachment to British partnership. Lend-Lease aid served American interests in preventing German control of European markets and resources. Intelligence cooperation provided Americans with access to European networks that proved valuable for post-war influence operations. Military coordination ensured American control over strategic decisions that shaped the post-war international order.

Contemporary American strategic documents rarely mention Britain except as one NATO ally among many, while British strategic documents consistently emphasize American partnership as central to British security and prosperity. This asymmetry reflects the actual balance of power and influence rather than the balanced partnership that British politicians claim to maintain. America shapes international events while Britain responds to American initiatives, hoping to influence outcomes through proximity to power rather than independent strategic capability.

The cost of this delusion extends beyond international embarrassment to domestic policy distortion that serves American rather than British interests. British foreign policy consistently prioritizes American preferences over European cooperation that might better serve British economic and security interests. British defence spending focuses on maintaining American interoperability rather than developing independent capabilities that might provide strategic autonomy. British economic policy accommodates American regulatory preferences while struggling to maintain relationships with European partners that represent larger markets and closer geographical proximity.

Until Britain acknowledges that the "special relationship" is a comforting fiction rather than strategic reality, British foreign policy will continue to serve American interests while failing to advance British priorities. The choice facing Britain is not between American partnership and European isolation, but between honest assessment of British capabilities and continued submission to American leadership disguised as special partnership. The relationship will remain special only in British imagination until Britain develops the strategic independence to make American partnership genuinely mutual rather than asymmetrically dependent.

The tragedy of the special relationship mythology is that it prevents Britain from developing the multilateral partnerships that might actually serve British interests in a world where American hegemony is declining and regional blocs are gaining influence. By clinging to the illusion of unique American partnership, Britain isolates itself from European cooperation, Asian economic growth, and African development opportunities that might provide genuine strategic alternatives to continued dependence on American goodwill that may not survive changes in American domestic politics or international priorities.

# Class Warfare: The Persistent Elite

British politicians from all parties recite the mantra that "we're all middle class now," celebrating the supposed death of the rigid class system that once defined British society. This comfortable fiction allows the establishment to claim that merit determines success while ignoring the overwhelming evidence that Britain remains one of the most class-stratified societies in the developed world. The old aristocratic titles may have lost their political power, but they have been replaced by an equally exclusive meritocratic elite that perpetuates privilege through educational advantages, social networks, and cultural capital that remain as impermeable to outsiders as any hereditary system.

The statistics demolish any pretence that Britain has become a classless society. According to Social Mobility Commission Reports from 2020-2024, social mobility in Britain has stagnated for the past three decades, with children from working-class backgrounds now less likely to achieve professional status than their counterparts were in the 1970s. Income inequality has increased substantially since the 1980s, while wealth concentration has reached levels not seen since the Edwardian era. The gap between rich and poor continues to widen despite decades of political rhetoric about opportunity and inclusion.

The persistence of class advantage is most starkly revealed in intergenerational earnings mobility data. Children from the top income quintile are fifteen times more likely to remain in the top quintile as adults than children from the bottom quintile are to reach it. This extraordinary lack of social mobility makes Britain one of the least meritocratic societies in the developed world, trailing behind not only Scandinavian countries but also France, Germany, and Canada in providing opportunities for advancement based on ability rather than background.

Private education provides the most obvious mechanism for perpetuating class advantage across generations. Private School Statistics from the Independent Schools Council (2024) reveal that just 7% of British children attend private schools, yet these institutions produce 74% of senior judges, 71% of senior military officers, 55% of permanent secretaries in the civil service, and 44% of members of parliament. This extraordinary overrepresentation cannot be explained by superior intelligence or harder work, but rather by the social networks, cultural confidence, and institutional connections that private education provides to those wealthy enough to purchase them.

The financial barriers to private education have increased dramatically over recent decades, making elite schooling even more exclusive than in previous generations. Average private school fees now exceed £15,000 annually, reaching over £40,000 at the most prestigious institutions when boarding costs are included. These fees have risen far faster than average incomes, ensuring that private education becomes increasingly concentrated among the wealthy rather than accessible to middle-class families seeking educational advantage for their children.

The examination of specific elite institutions reveals the mechanisms through which class privilege reproduces itself. Eton College alone has produced 20 British prime ministers, while comprehensive schools educating 93% of British children have produced exactly none. This is not coincidence but the result of systematic advantages that begin in childhood and compound throughout life. Eton pupils receive individual attention from masters with Oxford and Cambridge degrees, access to cultural experiences that broaden their horizons, and introduction to networks that will shape their entire careers.

Westminster School, Harrow, and other elite institutions operate as finishing schools for the ruling class, providing not just education but cultural formation that marks their graduates as belonging to the establishment. The curriculum includes subjects like classics and philosophy that have little practical application but serve as markers of elite culture. More importantly, these schools teach confidence, entitlement, and the social skills necessary for leadership in a society that continues to defer to upper-class authority.

Oxford and Cambridge universities, despite their claims about widening participation, continue to admit students from private schools at rates far exceeding their representation in the general population. According to 'The Class Ceiling' from the London School of Economics (2023), graduates from these institutions dominate not only politics and the civil service but also finance, media, and cultural institutions. The Oxbridge network operates as an informal recruiting system that ensures elite positions remain concentrated among those who attended the right institutions.

The admissions process at Oxford and Cambridge appears meritocratic while systematically favouring privileged applicants. Interview techniques, personal statements, and extracurricular achievements all depend on cultural capital that correlates strongly with class background. Students from state schools may achieve higher A-level grades but struggle with interview formats that assume familiarity with elite cultural references and communication styles. The result is that apparent academic merit often reflects economic advantage rather than innate ability.

Subject choice within elite universities further stratifies career opportunities along class lines. Philosophy, Politics, and Economics at Oxford, and similar courses at Cambridge, serve as pipelines to elite careers in politics, civil service, and finance. Working-class students who reach these universities often choose practical subjects like engineering or computer science that lead to professional employment but rarely to positions of social leadership. The most prestigious career paths remain concentrated among those who can afford to study subjects with limited immediate commercial application.

The legal profession demonstrates how professional meritocracy serves as a modern version of the old class system. Barristers must complete unpaid pupillages that only wealthy families can afford to subsidize, ensuring that working-class candidates are excluded regardless of ability. The requirement for expensive legal training, combined with the networking advantages that come from attending the right universities and dining at the right inns of court, creates barriers to entry that are as effective as any hereditary restriction.

The structure of legal careers reinforces these class advantages throughout professional development. Chambers operate through informal networks where work allocation depends on personal relationships and cultural fit rather than purely professional competence. Barristers from privileged backgrounds understand how to navigate these relationships, while working-class lawyers struggle with social codes they were never taught. The result is a legal system dominated by privately educated professionals who share similar backgrounds, perspectives, and social connections.

Judicial appointments reveal the ultimate outcome of these class dynamics within the legal profession. Senior judges are overwhelmingly products of private education and elite universities, creating a judiciary that shares common assumptions about society, justice, and appropriate behaviour. This concentration of power among the privileged has profound implications for how laws are interpreted and applied, particularly in cases involving class conflict or social inequality.

Financial services operate according to similar principles, with recruitment practices that Favor candidates from elite universities and privileged backgrounds. Investment banks and management consultancies explicitly target Oxford, Cambridge, and elite London universities while largely ignoring institutions that educate working-class students. The recruitment process emphasizes cultural fit and social confidence rather than technical competence, ensuring that financial power remains concentrated among those who already possess social advantages.

The culture of financial institutions reinforces class privilege through informal mechanisms that exclude working-class participants. After-work drinking, weekend social events, and expensive leisure activities serve as networking opportunities that shape career advancement. Working-class employees who cannot afford to participate in these activities or who feel uncomfortable in these social settings find themselves excluded from promotion opportunities despite their professional competence.

Compensation structures within financial services create additional barriers to working-class advancement. Unpaid internships, low starting salaries followed by large bonuses, and expectation of personal financial investment in professional development all Favor candidates whose families can provide financial support. Working-class graduates who need immediate income to support themselves or their families cannot afford the financial sacrifices that lead to long-term career success in these industries.

The media presents itself as a meritocratic industry where talent determines success, but examination of its leadership reveals the same patterns of class reproduction found elsewhere. Editors of major newspapers, controllers of television networks, and prominent journalists are overwhelmingly products of private education and elite universities. This concentration of cultural power among the privileged ensures that working-class perspectives are consistently marginalized while upper-class concerns receive disproportionate attention and sympathy.

Media recruitment operates through internship programs that systematically exclude working-class candidates through financial barriers and networking requirements. Unpaid work experience, lengthy application processes, and emphasis on cultural sophistication all Favor candidates whose families can provide both financial support and social connections. The result is newsrooms and production companies dominated by privileged graduates who share similar assumptions about what constitutes newsworthiness and cultural value.

Editorial decision-making reflects these class biases in subtle but pervasive ways. Stories about working-class communities are typically framed in terms of problems and pathology rather than strength and resilience. Middle-class concerns about house prices, school choice, and career advancement receive extensive coverage, while working-class issues like job security, wage stagnation, and public service cuts are treated as peripheral concerns. The media's class composition shapes not only what stories are told but how they are interpreted and presented to the public.

Political representation reflects these broader patterns of class dominance despite democratic elections that theoretically provide equal opportunity for participation. Income Inequality Data from the ONS (2024) shows that members of parliament are increasingly drawn from professional backgrounds rather than working-class occupations, even within the Labour Party that claims to represent working-class interests. The cost of political participation, from unpaid internships to campaign financing, favours candidates with independent wealth or family support that working-class aspirants cannot access.

The pathway to political prominence requires financial resources that exclude working-class candidates at multiple stages. University education, unpaid internships in political organizations, and years of voluntary campaigning all demand financial support that working-class families cannot provide. Even elected representatives face financial pressures that Favor those with independent wealth, as parliamentary salaries alone are insufficient to maintain the lifestyle expected of political leaders.

Political discourse reflects the class background of political elites through language, priorities, and assumptions that demonstrate distance from working-class experience. Debates about welfare policy, education reform, and economic development proceed without meaningful input from those most affected by these policies. The result is policy-making that serves the interests of the educated middle class while failing to address the concerns of working-class communities that feel increasingly disconnected from democratic representation.

The housing market has become perhaps the most important mechanism for transmitting class advantage across generations. Property ownership provides not only wealth accumulation but also access to better schools, safer neighbourhoods, and social networks that shape life opportunities. Young people from working-class families face house prices that require parental assistance most families cannot provide, while those from wealthy backgrounds receive deposits and guarantees that ensure continued geographic and social segregation.

Regional variations in property prices create additional dimensions of class stratification that reinforce existing inequalities. London and the South East offer the highest salaries and best career prospects, but housing costs ensure that these opportunities remain available primarily to those whose families can provide financial support. Working-class young people must choose between remaining in economically depressed areas or moving to expensive cities where they cannot afford to live.

The rental market operates as a mechanism for transferring wealth from working-class tenants to property-owning landlords, many of whom inherited their properties or purchased them with family assistance. Rising rents consume an increasing proportion of working-class incomes while providing investment returns for those wealthy enough to own multiple properties. This dynamic ensures that class advantages compound over time rather than diminishing through market mechanisms.

Cultural capital operates as a subtle but powerful force for maintaining class distinctions that appear to be based on individual preference rather than structural inequality. Knowledge of wine, art, literature, and classical music serves as a marker of elite status that influences employment decisions, social acceptance, and romantic partnerships. Working-class culture is consistently devalued while upper-class tastes are celebrated as sophisticated and refined, creating psychological barriers that complement the material obstacles facing those seeking social advancement.

Educational institutions play a crucial role in transmitting cultural capital by treating middle-class cultural knowledge as natural intelligence while dismissing working-class cultural knowledge as irrelevant or inferior. School curricula emphasize subjects and approaches that Favor students whose families possess books, cultural experiences, and educational values that align with institutional expectations. Students from working-class backgrounds are expected to abandon their cultural heritage and adopt middle-class values as the price of educational success.

The arts and cultural institutions reinforce these dynamics by celebrating forms of expression that require expensive training or sophisticated cultural knowledge while marginalizing popular culture associated with working-class communities. Opera, ballet, and classical music receive public subsidies and cultural prestige, while popular music, working men's clubs, and community festivals are treated as commercially driven entertainment rather than legitimate cultural expression.

Language and accent continue to serve as markers of class status that influence employment and social acceptance in ways that appear to be based on communication skills rather than prejudice. Received Pronunciation remains associated with intelligence and competence despite having no relationship to actual ability, while regional accents are perceived as indicating lower education and social status. These linguistic prejudices operate unconsciously in recruitment decisions, performance evaluations, and social interactions that shape life opportunities.

The broadcasting media reinforces these linguistic hierarchies by consistently featuring Received Pronunciation speakers in positions of authority while relegating regional accents to comedy, sports commentary, or human interest stories. This pattern teaches viewers to associate accent with social status and intellectual capacity, perpetuating prejudices that influence everything from job interviews to romantic relationships.

Educational achievement, supposedly the great equalizer in meritocratic society, actually reinforces class divisions through mechanisms that Favor privileged students while appearing to reward pure ability. Private schools provide smaller class sizes, better facilities, and more individual attention than state schools can afford. Wealthy families supplement school education with private tutoring, cultural experiences, and university preparation that working-class families cannot provide.

The examination system appears objective while systematically favouring students whose families understand how to prepare for standardized tests and navigate assessment requirements. Cultural knowledge, essay-writing skills, and test-taking strategies all correlate with class background rather than innate intelligence. Working-class students may possess equivalent ability but lack the cultural preparation necessary for academic success as currently measured.

University preparation requires financial resources and cultural knowledge that exclude working-class students from elite institutions regardless of their academic potential. Personal statements, extracurricular activities, and interview performance all depend on cultural capital that correlates strongly with class background. Even when universities attempt to correct for these advantages through contextual admissions policies, the fundamental dynamic remains unchanged because the entire system is designed around middle-class cultural assumptions.

Professional networking operates through informal mechanisms that exclude working-class participants while appearing to be based on personal compatibility rather than systematic discrimination. Alumni networks, professional associations, and social clubs provide access to job opportunities, business partnerships, and career advancement that formal qualifications alone cannot achieve. These networks operate through shared educational experiences, cultural references, and social connections that working-class professionals struggle to access regardless of their competence or achievements.

The Old Boys' Network remains active through alumni associations that provide career advantages to those who attended the right schools and universities. Former pupils of elite institutions maintain contact through organized events, professional associations, and social clubs that facilitate business relationships and employment opportunities. These networks operate openly while excluding those who did not attend elite institutions, creating parallel recruitment systems that bypass formal equal opportunity procedures.

Professional advancement increasingly depends on informal relationships developed through shared cultural experiences rather than workplace performance alone. Golf club memberships, wine society participation, and attendance at cultural events serve as networking opportunities that shape career development. Working-class professionals who cannot afford these activities or who feel uncomfortable in these settings find themselves excluded from advancement opportunities despite their professional competence.

Healthcare, supposedly provided equally through the NHS, actually reproduces class advantages through private options that wealthy families use to secure better treatment and faster access. Private health insurance, private consultations, and private hospitals provide superior care that ensures middle-class families maintain health advantages that translate into better life outcomes. Even within the NHS, middle-class patients receive better treatment through their ability to navigate the system, advocate for themselves, and access information about treatment options.

The two-tier healthcare system ensures that class advantages extend literally to matters of life and death. Cancer survival rates correlate with social class due to differences in early detection, treatment quality, and aftercare support. Mental health services are more readily available to those who can afford private treatment or who possess the cultural capital necessary to advocate effectively within NHS systems. These health inequalities compound other class disadvantages throughout life.

Nutrition and lifestyle choices that affect health outcomes are heavily influenced by class position through income constraints, educational differences, and cultural factors that shape behaviour. Fresh food, exercise facilities, and health information are more readily available to middle-class families, while working-class communities face food deserts, limited recreational opportunities, and health messaging that fails to address structural constraints on healthy choices.

Geographic segregation reinforces class divisions by concentrating different social groups in separate residential areas with distinct educational, commercial, and cultural institutions. Middle-class areas feature better schools, more cultural amenities, and stronger social networks, while working-class areas struggle with underinvestment, social problems, and limited opportunities for advancement. This spatial separation ensures that class differences are reinforced through daily experience rather than challenged through social mixing.

School catchment areas operate as mechanisms for reproducing class advantage through property markets that exclude working-class families from areas with high-performing schools. Middle-class families strategically purchase homes near successful schools, driving up property prices and ensuring that educational opportunities remain concentrated among those who can afford expensive housing. This dynamic creates educational inequality that appears to be based on parental choice rather than systematic exclusion.

The retail and service economies that dominate working-class areas provide different goods, services, and employment opportunities than those available in middle-class neighbourhoods. Payday lenders, betting shops, and fast food outlets cluster in working-class areas, while middle-class areas feature banks, professional services, and healthy food options. These differences shape life opportunities and reinforce class distinctions through environmental factors that appear to reflect personal choice rather than structural inequality.

Political discourse about class deliberately obscures these realities through language that emphasizes individual responsibility while ignoring structural constraints that shape life opportunities. The concept of meritocracy serves as ideological justification for inequality by suggesting that success reflects personal virtue rather than inherited advantage. This narrative allows the privileged to feel good about their position while blaming the disadvantaged for their circumstances.

The rhetoric of social mobility serves similar ideological functions by suggesting that individual advancement is possible while ignoring the mathematical impossibility of universal upward mobility in hierarchical systems. Politicians celebrate exceptional cases of working-class success while ignoring the systemic barriers that make such success rare. This focus on individual achievement obscures the structural changes necessary to create genuine equality of opportunity.

Policy responses to class inequality consistently focus on changing individual behaviour rather than addressing institutional arrangements that perpetuate privilege. Education policy emphasizes raising aspirations and improving skills while ignoring the cultural and economic barriers that prevent working-class advancement. Employment policy promotes entrepreneurship and self-improvement while maintaining economic structures that concentrate wealth and opportunity among existing elites.

The Brexit referendum revealed the class dynamics underlying British politics when working-class voters used the opportunity to express frustration with an establishment that had ignored their interests for decades. The remain campaign was dominated by upper-class voices that dismissed working-class concerns as ignorance or prejudice, confirming the class contempt that fuels popular resentment of elite dominance. The subsequent political response has focused on managing this rebellion rather than addressing its underlying causes.

The cultural response to Brexit demonstrated the establishment's inability to understand working-class grievances as legitimate political concerns rather than expressions of ignorance or bigotry. Media coverage portrayed Leave voters as uneducated and backward, while Remain voters were presented as informed and cosmopolitan. This framing revealed the class prejudices that shape elite attitudes toward democratic participation by those outside their social circle.

Post-Brexit political developments have confirmed working-class suspicions about elite intentions by pursuing policies that serve professional class interests while ignoring working-class concerns about immigration, job security, and community stability. The political establishment has treated the referendum result as a problem to be managed rather than a mandate for change, demonstrating the limited nature of democratic accountability in a class-stratified society.

Modern British society has achieved the remarkable feat of maintaining rigid class hierarchy while denying its existence, creating a system more insidious than traditional aristocracy because it appears to be based on merit rather than birth. The old class system was at least honest about its exclusions, while the new meritocracy pretends that anyone can succeed while ensuring that advantage continues to flow to those who already possess it.

The meritocratic ideology serves multiple functions for the privileged classes by justifying their advantages while obscuring the mechanisms through which those advantages operate. Successful individuals can attribute their achievements to personal virtue rather than structural privilege, while unsuccessful individuals can be blamed for their failures rather than supported through social solidarity. This individualization of social outcomes serves elite interests by preventing collective action to address systematic inequality.

Until Britain acknowledges that class remains the primary determinant of life opportunities, attempts at social reform will continue to fail because they address symptoms rather than causes. The fiction that Britain has become a classless society serves the interests of those who benefit from continued inequality while preventing honest discussion of the structural changes needed to create genuine equality of opportunity. The class war continues, but only one side admits to fighting it.

# Weather: The Great Distraction

British obsession with weather conversation represents the triumph of trivial preoccupation over serious discourse, a national fixation that serves as the perfect metaphor for Britain's inability to address genuine problems. No other developed nation devotes such intellectual energy to discussing meteorological conditions that are both predictable and mild, yet British culture treats weather commentary as sophisticated social interaction rather than conversational bankruptcy. This obsession reveals a society so uncomfortable with meaningful discussion that it has elevated small talk about rain to the status of cultural institution.

The statistical reality of British weather exposes the absurdity of national preoccupation with climatic conditions that barely qualify as noteworthy by international standards. UK Climate Data from the Met Office (2024) reveals temperature variations that rarely exceed 30 degrees Celsius in summer or fall below minus 10 degrees Celsius in winter, making Britain one of the most climatically stable regions in the world. Annual rainfall averages between 800 and 1,400 millimetres, distributed relatively evenly throughout the year without the dramatic seasonal variations that characterize genuinely challenging climates.

International Weather Comparisons from the World Meteorological Organization (2023) place British weather among the most benign on earth, lacking the hurricanes, tornadoes, droughts, floods, monsoons, or extreme temperatures that regularly devastate other regions. Britain experiences no significant natural disasters, no life-threatening seasonal variations, and no weather patterns that materially impact daily life beyond the trivial inconvenience of carrying an umbrella. Yet British conversation treats these mild variations as subjects worthy of endless analysis and commentary.

The geographical reality makes British weather obsession even more inexplicable. Britain is a small island nation where weather conditions remain relatively uniform across the entire territory, making regional weather variations minimal compared to continental countries that experience genuinely diverse climatic zones. A storm system crossing Britain takes hours rather than days, seasonal changes occur gradually without dramatic transitions, and extreme weather events are so rare that they generate major news coverage when they occur.

The predictability of British weather patterns undermines claims that weather uncertainty justifies constant discussion. Seasonal variations follow established patterns that have remained consistent for centuries, with summer temperatures slightly warmer than winter temperatures and rainfall distributed throughout the year. Weather forecasting technology provides accurate predictions several days in advance, making weather-related planning straightforward for anyone capable of basic preparation.

Yet British culture has constructed an elaborate mythology around weather unpredictability that serves as justification for obsessive meteorological commentary. The phrase "if you don't like the weather, wait five minutes" is repeated as if it represents profound insight rather than meaningless cliché applicable to any location on earth. This supposed unpredictability is cited as evidence of British weather's unique character, when in fact British weather is notably more stable and predictable than most global regions.

The social function of weather conversation reveals its true purpose as sophisticated avoidance mechanism that allows British people to interact without engaging in meaningful discourse.

Weather provides safe conversational territory that avoids controversial topics, personal revelations, or intellectual challenge while maintaining the appearance of social engagement. This cultural preference for superficial interaction over substantive discussion reflects broader British tendencies toward emotional repression and conflict avoidance.

The linguistic elaboration of weather vocabulary demonstrates the cultural energy devoted to this fundamentally trivial subject. British English contains dozens of words for precipitation, temperature, and atmospheric conditions that serve no practical purpose beyond allowing speakers to demonstrate cultural competence in meteorological discourse. Terms like "drizzle," "spitting," "chucking it down," and "brass monkeys" create the illusion of precision while describing variations too subtle to affect behaviour or planning.

Regional variations in weather terminology provide additional opportunities for cultural display that substitute local knowledge for genuine expertise. Scottish, Welsh, Northern English, and Southern English dialects maintain distinct weather vocabularies that allow speakers to signal regional identity through meteorological commentary. This linguistic diversity creates the false impression that different parts of Britain experience meaningfully different weather conditions rather than minor variations in timing and intensity.

The temporal structure of British weather obsession reveals its function as conversational filler rather than information exchange. Weather conversations follow predictable patterns: observation of current conditions, comparison with recent conditions, speculation about future conditions, and expression of satisfaction or dissatisfaction with meteorological developments. This ritualistic format allows participants to demonstrate social competence without contributing meaningful content to human interaction.

The seasonal cycle of weather complaints provides year-round opportunities for meteorological grievance that substitute emotional expression for practical problem-solving. Summer temperatures above 25 degrees Celsius generate complaints about excessive heat, while winter temperatures below 5 degrees Celsius produce protests about bitter cold. Spring rainfall prompts commentary about wetness, while autumn winds occasion observations about gustiness. These complaints serve no practical purpose beyond providing socially acceptable outlets for general dissatisfaction.

The infrastructure implications of British weather obsession reveal massive resource misallocation driven by cultural mythology rather than practical necessity. Transport systems designed to cope with "extreme" weather conditions that occur rarely and cause minimal disruption consume resources that could address genuine infrastructure needs. Snow preparation for weather events that affect Britain perhaps once annually costs millions of pounds while rail services fail daily due to "leaves on the line" and "wrong kind of snow."

School closures for weather conditions that children in other countries navigate routinely demonstrate how weather mythology justifies institutional dysfunction. Light snowfall that would be considered normal winter conditions in most northern countries triggers educational disruption in Britain, depriving children of learning opportunities while creating childcare crises for working parents. These closures reflect cultural hypersensitivity to minor weather variations rather than genuine safety concerns.

Media coverage of weather events reveals the cultural displacement of genuine news priorities in Favor of meteorological drama. Weather stories dominate headlines during periods when more significant political, economic, and social developments receive minimal attention. "Weather warnings" for conditions that require no behavioural modification beyond wearing appropriate clothing are treated as major news events, while substantive policy failures that affect millions of lives are relegated to inside pages.

The economic impact of weather obsession extends beyond infrastructure spending to productivity losses caused by cultural permission to treat minor weather variations as legitimate excuses for reduced performance. "Too hot to work" complaints during summer temperatures that workers in genuinely hot climates consider normal provide socially acceptable justification for decreased effort. Similarly, winter weather that barely requires additional clothing becomes grounds for tardiness, absenteeism, and general underperformance.

The psychological function of weather conversation serves as projection mechanism for emotional states that British culture otherwise discourages people from expressing directly. Complaints about gloomy weather provide acceptable outlets for depression, while celebration of sunny days allows expressions of joy that might otherwise seem inappropriate. This emotional displacement prevents genuine processing of psychological states while maintaining the illusion of stoic emotional control.

The international perception of British weather obsession damages national reputation more than actual climatic conditions could ever achieve. Foreign visitors consistently express bewilderment at British weather conversation, recognizing it as cultural quirk rather than response to genuine environmental challenge. This reputation for meteorological preoccupation reinforces stereotypes about British inability to engage with substantial issues, contributing to international perceptions of decline and irrelevance.

The historical context of weather obsession reveals its development as cultural compensation for loss of empire and international significance. When Britain controlled global territories experiencing genuinely diverse and challenging climates, weather conversation focused on exotic conditions in distant locations. As imperial reach contracted, weather discourse contracted to local conditions, transforming from genuine environmental awareness to parochial preoccupation with trivial variations.

The class dimensions of weather conversation provide opportunities for social distinction based on meteorological sophistication that substitute cultural capital for genuine expertise. Knowledge of regional weather patterns, seasonal variations, and historical weather events allows speakers to demonstrate local knowledge and cultural competence. Weather conversation becomes performance of belonging that excludes outsiders while creating false impression of shared community interest.

The agricultural justification for weather attention has become largely irrelevant in post-industrial Britain where less than 2% of employment involves farming, yet weather conversation continues as if the entire population depends on precipitation patterns for survival. This anachronistic focus reflects cultural inability to adapt social customs to contemporary economic reality, maintaining rural preoccupations in urban society that has lost connection with land-based production.

The seasonal affective aspects of weather discussion provide medical justification for emotional responses to climatic conditions that are too mild to affect psychological wellbeing significantly. Claims about depression caused by winter darkness ignore the reality that British winter days provide several hours of daylight and that artificial lighting easily compensates for reduced natural illumination. These pseudo-medical explanations legitimize emotional responses that reflect broader life dissatisfaction rather than genuine environmental sensitivity.

The technological revolution in weather prediction and climate control has eliminated most practical reasons for weather conversation, yet cultural obsession continues undiminished. Indoor climate control, accurate forecasting, and appropriate clothing make weather variations irrelevant to daily life for most British people, while weather conversation increases rather than decreases. This disconnect between practical necessity and cultural preoccupation reveals the purely social function of meteorological discourse.

The sports and leisure justification for weather attention applies to minimal percentage of time and activities for most British people, yet weather conversation proceeds as if outdoor recreation dominates national life. Professional sports continue regardless of weather conditions, while most leisure activities occur indoors or can be easily modified to accommodate climatic variations. The alleged impact of weather on recreational planning serves as convenient excuse for social inactivity rather than genuine constraint on lifestyle choices.

The gardening rationale for weather consciousness affects limited portion of British population and requires only basic meteorological awareness rather than obsessive daily commentary. Professional landscapers and serious gardeners understand seasonal patterns without need for constant weather discussion, while casual gardeners can address plant care through simple observation and basic preparation. Weather conversation far exceeds any practical gardening requirements.

The health justifications for weather preoccupation lack medical foundation for conditions as mild as those experienced in Britain. Temperature variations that require no behavioural modification beyond clothing selection are treated as health threats, while genuinely dangerous environmental conditions like air pollution receive minimal attention. This misallocation of health concern reflects cultural mythology rather than medical evidence.

The travel implications of weather concern apply to minority of British activities yet dominate conversational attention disproportionate to actual impact. Modern transportation systems operate effectively in all normal British weather conditions, while travel disruption typically results from inadequate infrastructure investment rather than challenging weather. Weather-related travel conversation serves as socially acceptable complaint mechanism rather than response to genuine inconvenience.

The cultural export of British weather obsession through media and literature has created international awareness of this quirk without inspiring emulation, suggesting recognition of its fundamental absurdity. British weather conversation appears in foreign depictions of British culture as comedic element rather than admirable tradition, reinforcing international perceptions of British eccentricity and irrelevance.

The environmental movement has provided new justification for weather attention through climate change concerns that confuse local weather variations with global climate patterns. This confusion allows weather obsession to appear environmentally conscious while actually demonstrating inability to distinguish between daily weather fluctuations and long-term climate trends. Weather conversation continues to focus on immediate local conditions rather than genuine environmental challenges.

The social media amplification of weather conversation has expanded traditional limitations on meteorological discourse while revealing its essential vacuity when subjected to written analysis. Twitter feeds devoted to weather commentary expose the repetitive and meaningless nature of weather conversation when removed from immediate social context. The written form reveals weather discussion as content-free social ritual rather than information exchange.

The therapeutic industry has embraced weather sensitivity as legitimate psychological condition requiring professional attention, medicalizing normal responses to minor environmental variations. Weather-related therapy sessions focus on managing emotional responses to climatic conditions too mild to affect wellbeing, while genuine psychological issues receive inadequate attention. This medicalization of weather sensitivity reflects broader cultural tendency to pathologize normal human variation.

The educational system incorporates weather studies into curricula despite limited practical application for most career paths, while neglecting subjects with genuine utility for adult life. Geography lessons devoted to British weather patterns consume time that could address more relevant topics, while meteorology receives attention disproportionate to its economic importance.

This educational emphasis reinforces cultural weather obsession while failing to prepare students for practical challenges.

Until Britain recognizes weather conversation as symptomatic of cultural inability to engage with substantial issues, this obsession will continue to substitute meteorological trivia for meaningful social interaction. The choice facing British society is between continued preoccupation with climatic conditions that barely affect daily life and development of conversational culture capable of addressing genuine challenges facing the nation. Weather talk serves as perfect metaphor for British decline: endless commentary about trivial variations while ignoring fundamental problems requiring serious attention and practical solutions.

The great irony of British weather obsession is that it has become the most predictable aspect of British culture, following patterns more consistent than the weather it claims to discuss. This cultural ritual will continue regardless of actual climatic conditions because it serves psychological and social functions unrelated to meteorological reality, providing safe conversational territory for people too uncomfortable with genuine discourse to risk meaningful human interaction.

# The Queue Mythology

British pride in queuing represents perhaps the most ridiculous aspect of national self-mythology, a celebration of standing in orderly lines that reveals profound confusion between courtesy and competence, patience and passivity. This cultural fixation treats the ability to wait without complaint as evidence of superior civilization, when in fact it demonstrates acceptance of inefficient service delivery that other developed nations would find intolerable. The mythology of British queuing excellence serves as perfect metaphor for national decline: taking pride in managing failure rather than demanding success.

The statistical reality of British service quality demolishes any legitimate basis for queuing pride. Customer Service Rankings from the Institute of Customer Service (2024) place Britain near the bottom of developed country comparisons for service efficiency, responsiveness, and customer satisfaction. What British culture celebrates as admirable patience, other nations recognize as evidence of systematic service failure that competent organizations would address rather than expect customers to endure.

Transport systems provide the most obvious evidence of British service inadequacy disguised as queuing virtue. Network Rail statistics from 2024 reveal chronic delays, cancellations, and overcrowding that force passengers to queue not because they choose orderly behaviour but because inadequate infrastructure provides no alternative. German, Swiss, and Japanese transport systems achieve superior reliability without requiring passengers to demonstrate stoic acceptance of regular service failure.

The London Underground, supposedly a model of urban transport efficiency, operates with delays and disruptions that would trigger government collapse in countries with genuine transport competence. Passengers queue for platforms because trains arrive late, queue for carriages because services are overcrowded, and queue for exits because infrastructure cannot handle passenger volumes efficiently. This is not evidence of British courtesy but proof of systematic underinvestment in transport capacity.

International Service Quality Comparisons from J.D. Power (2023) reveal that British consumers wait longer, receive slower service, and experience more service failures than their counterparts in other developed countries. What appears to British observers as admirable patience appears to international observers as inexplicable tolerance for incompetence. British queuing culture has evolved to manage service failure rather than demand service excellence.

The healthcare queuing mythology provides even starker evidence of British confusion between virtue and dysfunction. NHS waiting rooms operate as monuments to service failure disguised as patient consideration, where people queue for hours to receive medical attention that other healthcare systems provide efficiently. The ability to wait stoically for inadequate healthcare is celebrated as British virtue rather than recognized as evidence of systematic healthcare failure.

Emergency department queues that extend for twelve hours or more represent healthcare collapse, not cultural achievement. Patients die waiting for treatment that efficient healthcare systems would provide immediately, while British culture treats this deadly inefficiency as evidence of egalitarian healthcare principles. The mythology transforms healthcare failure into healthcare virtue through cultural gymnastics that prioritize ideological comfort over patient outcomes.

Appointment systems that require patients to queue for access to their own healthcare create multiple layers of inefficiency that competent systems would eliminate through proper resource allocation and scheduling technology. Patients queue to make appointments, queue to check in for appointments, queue to see healthcare providers, and queue to collect prescriptions. Each queue represents a point of service failure disguised as organizational necessity.

Retail queuing demonstrates how British businesses exploit cultural tolerance for inefficiency to reduce staffing costs while maintaining profit margins. Supermarket chains deliberately understaffed checkout areas because British consumers will queue rather than demand adequate service levels. This cultural acceptance of inconvenience allows businesses to externalize their operational costs onto customers who provide free labour through queuing time.

The contrast with retail operations in other countries reveals the artificial nature of British queuing acceptance. German supermarkets achieve faster checkout times through adequate staffing and efficient processes, while British supermarkets rely on customer patience to manage inadequate service provision. Self-checkout systems that create additional queuing while reducing employment represent the logical conclusion of this service degradation disguised as technological progress.

Banking services exploit queuing culture to reduce costs while maintaining the appearance of personal service through inefficient branch operations that could be eliminated through proper technology investment. Customers queue for services that could be provided instantly through digital platforms, while banks profit from maintaining expensive physical infrastructure that serves no practical purpose beyond preserving jobs for middle management.

The technological solutions that eliminate queuing in other countries remain underutilized in Britain because queuing culture provides psychological comfort for both service providers and consumers. Appointment systems, online booking, and efficient scheduling would eliminate most queuing scenarios, but British organizations resist implementing systems that would reveal the extent of their operational inefficiency.

Government services provide spectacular examples of queuing mythology disguising administrative incompetence. Citizens queue for passport applications, driving license renewals, and benefit assessments that other countries process efficiently through online systems. The queues exist not because personal interaction is necessary but because government departments lack the competence to implement efficient service delivery.

Post office queues represent the final degradation of a service that once functioned efficiently but has been deliberately crippled through privatization and cost-cutting. Customers queue for basic postal services that other countries provide quickly and efficiently, while the mythology celebrates patient acceptance of service failure rather than demanding restoration of functional postal services.

The psychological dimension of queuing reveals its function as social control mechanism that channels frustration into passive acceptance rather than active demand for improvement. Queuing culture teaches people to accept inefficiency as inevitable rather than challenge inadequate service provision. This psychological conditioning serves the interests of incompetent service providers while training citizens to lower their expectations rather than demand competence.

The social stratification of queuing exposes the class dimensions underlying apparently egalitarian queuing culture. Wealthy individuals avoid queues through premium services, private healthcare, business class travel, and personal assistance, while working-class citizens queue for basic services that middle-class people purchase privately. The mythology of egalitarian queuing conceals the reality that queuing culture primarily affects those unable to purchase alternatives.

Professional-class workers rarely experience the queuing that dominates working-class service experiences because their employment provides access to private alternatives or because their cultural capital allows them to navigate systems more efficiently. The celebration of queuing culture comes primarily from people who experience queuing occasionally rather than those for whom queuing represents routine frustration with inadequate service provision.

The international perception of British queuing culture damages national reputation more than any supposed civility could enhance it. Foreign business people recognize queuing tolerance as evidence of low service standards rather than admirable cultural trait. This reputation for accepting inefficiency discourages international investment and reinforces perceptions of British economic decline.

Tourist experiences of British queuing reveal the gap between mythology and reality. Visitors expect efficient service based on advanced economy status but encounter queuing culture that suggests developing country service standards. The contrast between British self-perception and international experience contributes to disappointing tourism experiences that damage the service economy.

The historical development of queuing culture reflects post-war rationing and resource scarcity that created temporary necessity for orderly resource distribution. What began as practical response to genuine scarcity became cultural habit that persisted long after the material conditions that justified it had disappeared. Contemporary queuing culture represents cultural fossilization rather than adaptive social behaviour.

Wartime queuing served legitimate purposes when resources were genuinely scarce and fair distribution required organized allocation systems. Citizens queued for rationed goods because alternative distribution methods would have created greater inequity and social conflict. This historical context provided rational foundation for queuing behaviour that contemporary service failures do not justify.

The transition from necessity-based queuing to cultural choice reveals how temporary adaptations become permanent cultural features that outlive their practical justification. Post-war reconstruction could have prioritized efficient service delivery, but instead normalized queuing culture that excused continued service inadequacy. This cultural path dependency trapped Britain in inefficient service patterns that other countries avoided through different developmental choices.

The economic cost of queuing culture includes both direct time costs for individuals and indirect economic costs from reduced productivity and inefficient resource allocation. Time spent queuing represents economic waste that efficient service provision would eliminate, while businesses that exploit queuing tolerance operate less efficiently than competitors who must provide better service to retain customers.

Productivity calculations that include queuing time reveal substantial economic losses from service inefficiency disguised as cultural virtue. Workers who spend lunch hours queuing for basic services return to work frustrated and depleted, while efficient service provision would allow productive use of break time. These individual productivity losses aggregate into significant economic drag that efficient service countries avoid.

The opportunity cost of queuing extends beyond immediate time loss to include the psychological and physical stress that inefficient service provision creates. People who queue regularly experience frustration, fatigue, and resentment that affect their broader life satisfaction and social relationships. Efficient service provision would improve quality of life while reducing social tension and interpersonal conflict.

The technological obsolescence of most queuing scenarios makes continued tolerance for queuing evidence of institutional failure rather than cultural sophistication. Digital appointment systems, online service provision, and automated processing could eliminate most queuing while improving service quality and reducing costs. The persistence of queuing culture prevents adoption of efficient technologies that would benefit both providers and consumers.

Artificial intelligence and automation could revolutionize service delivery by predicting demand, optimizing scheduling, and personalizing service provision in ways that would eliminate queuing while improving customer satisfaction. British resistance to these technological solutions reflects cultural attachment to inefficient traditions rather than commitment to service excellence.

The environmental impact of queuing includes energy consumption from maintaining physical queuing spaces, transportation emissions from unnecessary journeys, and resource waste from inefficient service provision. Digital service delivery would reduce environmental impact while improving service quality, but queuing culture prevents adoption of environmentally superior alternatives.

The social justice implications of queuing culture reveal its regressive impact on people with disabilities, elderly citizens, and working parents who cannot afford the time cost that queuing imposes. Efficient service provision would improve access for vulnerable populations, while queuing culture creates barriers that discriminate against those who cannot easily navigate inefficient service systems.

Parents with young children, people with mobility limitations, and workers with inflexible schedules suffer disproportionately from queuing requirements that assume universal ability to wait indefinitely for service. The mythology of egalitarian queuing conceals the reality that queuing culture discriminates against those whose circumstances require efficient service provision.

The democratic implications of queuing culture extend beyond service delivery to broader patterns of political passivity that accept institutional failure rather than demand governmental competence. Citizens who queue patiently for basic services are conditioned to accept inefficient governance rather than hold public institutions accountable for performance failures.

Political queuing during elections creates the absurd spectacle of citizens queuing to exercise democratic rights in countries where efficient voting systems would eliminate delays. This combination of democratic participation with service inefficiency sends contradictory messages about governmental competence and civic engagement.

The international competitiveness implications of queuing culture include reduced attractiveness for international business investment, tourism disappointment, and brain drain as talented individuals choose countries with more efficient service provision. Nations that prioritize service efficiency attract economic activity that Britain loses through acceptance of service inadequacy.

The educational implications of queuing culture include teaching children to accept inefficiency as normal rather than demanding excellence from institutions and service providers. Schools that require students to queue for lunch, restrooms, and administrative services train future citizens to tolerate service failure rather than expect institutional competence.

University queuing for registration, accommodation, and student services introduces international students to British service standards that compare unfavourably with their home countries. This early exposure to queuing culture creates negative impressions that affect decisions about remaining in Britain for employment or further education.

The healthcare implications of queuing culture extend beyond direct medical delays to include psychological stress, physical discomfort, and family disruption that inefficient healthcare delivery creates. Patients who must queue for medical attention experience additional health burdens that efficient healthcare systems would prevent.

Mental health impacts of chronic queuing include anxiety, depression, and learned helplessness that affect broader life satisfaction and social functioning. People who regularly experience service failure through queuing develop expectation of institutional incompetence that affects their willingness to engage with service providers and seek assistance when needed.

Until Britain recognizes queuing culture as evidence of service failure rather than cultural virtue, the nation will continue to accept inefficiency that other countries would find intolerable. The choice facing Britain is between continued celebration of managed decline through queuing mythology and development of service standards that prioritize efficiency over tradition. Queuing culture serves as perfect symbol of British acceptance of failure disguised as virtue, preventing the service improvements that would enhance quality of life while improving economic competitiveness.

The great irony of British queuing pride is that it celebrates passivity in the face of problems that active engagement could solve, transforming a response to temporary scarcity into permanent acceptance of artificial inefficiency. Until British culture learns to demand service excellence rather than celebrate service tolerance, queuing will continue to symbolize national decline disguised as cultural achievement.

# The Customer Service Con

The ubiquitous "zero tolerance to abuse" signs adorning every British business premises represent one of the most cynical exercises in corporate gaslighting ever perpetrated on a consumer population. These notices, prominently displayed in locations where customer service ranges from indifferent to actively hostile, serve as pre-emptive strikes against legitimate consumer complaints while protecting businesses from accountability for deliberately degraded service standards. The signs create a parallel universe where companies systematically abuse customers through incompetence and cost-cutting, then claim victim status when customers express predictable frustration with service that would shame a developing nation.

The timing of these signs reveals their true purpose as corporate shields rather than genuine worker protection. They proliferated during the same period when businesses deliberately cut staffing levels, outsourced customer service to distant call centres, and implemented automated systems designed to frustrate customers into abandoning legitimate complaints. The correlation between service degradation and abuse warnings exposes the cynical calculation behind this strategy: create conditions guaranteed to generate customer frustration, then criminalize the predictable emotional responses.

Customer Complaint Statistics from the Financial Ombudsman (2024) reveal the scale of systematic service failure that necessitates these defensive measures. British consumers file more complaints per capita than citizens of any comparable developed nation, not because British customers are uniquely difficult but because British service standards have collapsed to levels that generate inevitable frustration. The complaints data shows consistent patterns of service failure across industries, demonstrating that poor service is strategic choice rather than operational accident.

The specific language of these warnings reveals their function as psychological manipulation rather than legitimate workplace protection. Phrases like "our staff have the right to work without abuse" create false moral equivalence between service providers who choose to deliver inadequate service and customers who involuntarily receive it. This framing positions businesses as victims while casting customers as potential aggressors, inverting the actual power relationship between organizations and individuals seeking basic service competence.

The definition of "abuse" employed by these policies expands legitimate workplace protection into censorship of consumer criticism, treating expressions of dissatisfaction as personal attacks rather than service feedback. Raised voices, frustrated language, and persistent requests for resolution are classified as abusive behaviour, while systematic service failure that wastes customer time and money receives no comparable classification. This asymmetrical definition protects businesses from accountability while exposing customers to arbitrary exclusion from services they require.

Training programs that accompany these policies focus on identifying customer "aggression" rather than preventing service failures that create customer frustration. Staff receive detailed instruction on recognizing "difficult" customers while receiving minimal training on delivering competent service that would eliminate most customer complaints. This training priority reveals that businesses view customer frustration as inevitable rather than preventable, suggesting systematic intention to provide inadequate service.

The enforcement of abuse policies demonstrates their selective application designed to silence legitimate complaints rather than protect workers from genuine harassment. Customers who politely accept poor service rarely encounter policy enforcement, while those who persist in seeking resolution face escalating restrictions regardless of their behaviour. This selective enforcement reveals that the policies target effective complaint behaviour rather than actually abusive conduct.

Call centre operations provide the most egregious examples of systematic customer abuse disguised as service provision. Companies deliberately design phone systems to frustrate callers through endless menu options, hold times measured in hours, and repeated transfers between departments. These systems serve no operational purpose beyond discouraging customer contact, yet businesses claim victim status when customers express predictable frustration with obviously deliberate obstruction.

The geographic displacement of customer service through offshore call centres represents industrial-scale customer abuse that receives no acknowledgment in corporate abuse policies. Customers seeking support for British services must navigate language barriers, cultural disconnects, and time zone complications that create additional frustration beyond the original service problem. This systematic degradation of customer communication serves no purpose beyond cost reduction at customer expense.

Automated customer service systems that trap customers in recursive loops demonstrate corporate contempt for customer time and needs that violates any reasonable definition of respectful treatment. Interactive voice response systems that fail to recognize common requests, chatbots that provide irrelevant responses, and online forms that reject valid submissions create deliberate barriers to problem resolution. These systems abuse customers systematically while maintaining corporate deniability about service quality.

The retail implementation of abuse policies creates asymmetrical power relationships where businesses can exclude customers arbitrarily while customers have no recourse against service failures. Shop staff who provide incorrect information, ignore customer requests, or display obvious incompetence face no consequences, while customers who express dissatisfaction risk permanent exclusion from services they require. This power imbalance transforms commercial transactions into exercises in corporate dominance rather than mutual exchange.

Self-checkout systems represent the logical conclusion of customer service degradation, forcing customers to perform labour previously done by employees while maintaining the fiction that this represents improved service. Customers who struggle with deliberately counterintuitive systems are blamed for technical failures designed to frustrate users, while businesses profit from eliminating employment while maintaining prices. The abuse policies protect these systems from criticism by framing customer frustration as unreasonable behaviour.

Banking services demonstrate how abuse policies protect systematic customer exploitation through fee structures and service restrictions designed to generate revenue through customer confusion and inconvenience. Banks deliberately complicate simple transactions, impose arbitrary restrictions on account access, and charge fees for services that cost nothing to provide. When customers object to these practices, abuse policies silence criticism while protecting exploitative business models.

Insurance companies employ abuse policies to protect claim denial strategies that systematically breach contract obligations while avoiding customer accountability. Legitimate claims are rejected through bureaucratic obstruction, policy interpretation games, and deliberate delay tactics designed to force customer abandonment. Customers who persist in seeking contracted benefits face escalating hostility disguised as abuse prevention, while companies profit from breach of contract.

Utility companies use abuse policies to shield monopolistic service practices that exploit captive customer bases through deliberate inefficiency and arbitrary policy enforcement. Customers who cannot switch providers must accept service failures that competitive markets would eliminate, while abuse policies prevent criticism of practices that would be commercially impossible in genuinely competitive industries.

The legal framework surrounding abuse policies provides businesses with arbitrary power to exclude customers without appeal or accountability, creating commercial relationships that violate basic consumer protection principles. Customers banned under abuse policies have no right to appeal, no requirement for evidence, and no recourse against false accusations. This legal asymmetry transforms commercial relationships into exercises in corporate authority rather than mutual obligation.

Consumer protection agencies that should challenge abusive business practices instead validate abuse policies by treating them as legitimate workplace protection rather than consumer manipulation. Regulatory bodies investigate individual consumer complaints while ignoring systematic patterns of service failure that generate predictable customer frustration. This regulatory capture protects businesses from accountability while abandoning consumers to arbitrary corporate power.

The psychological impact of abuse policies extends beyond immediate service interactions to broader conditioning that teaches consumers to accept inadequate service rather than demand competence. Customers who fear exclusion modify their behaviour to accommodate business incompetence, creating learned helplessness that serves corporate interests while degrading consumer confidence and social trust.

The social stratification of abuse policy enforcement reveals their discriminatory impact on vulnerable populations who cannot easily access alternative service providers. Elderly customers, people with disabilities, and those with limited technological skills suffer disproportionately from service failures while facing greater risk of exclusion under abuse policies. This discrimination violates equality principles while protecting businesses from serving difficult customer populations.

Working-class customers experience abuse policy enforcement more frequently than middle-class customers who possess cultural capital and economic alternatives that provide protection against arbitrary exclusion. The policies effectively criminalize working-class expressions of frustration while tolerating middle-class complaint styles that conform to corporate expectations about appropriate customer behaviour.

The international comparison reveals that abuse policies are uniquely British responses to service failures that other countries address through genuine service improvement. European businesses achieve higher customer satisfaction without requiring abuse policies because they invest in service competence rather than customer management. This comparison exposes British abuse policies as symptoms of systematic service failure rather than responses to uniquely difficult customers.

American businesses that employ similar abuse rhetoric operate in competitive markets where service failures result in customer defection, creating natural limits on corporate abuse of customer relationships. British businesses exploit captive customer bases and limited competition to implement abuse policies that would be commercially impossible in genuinely competitive markets.

The technological solutions that could eliminate most service failures remain unimplemented because abuse policies provide cheaper alternatives to service investment. Businesses prefer customer management through abuse policies to service improvement through better systems, staffing, and processes. This choice reveals that poor service is strategic decision rather than operational constraint.

Artificial intelligence and automation could resolve most customer service issues instantly and accurately, but businesses resist implementing solutions that would eliminate opportunities for cost-cutting through service degradation. The persistence of inefficient service systems demonstrates corporate preference for managing customer frustration rather than preventing it.

The economic cost of abuse policies includes reduced consumer confidence, decreased economic activity, and productivity losses from service inefficiency that affects broader economic performance. Customers who avoid businesses due to poor service reduce economic activity while spreading negative experiences that damage business reputations and industry confidence.

The tourism impact of British customer service standards damages international reputation and reduces foreign visitor satisfaction with British commercial experiences. International visitors accustomed to competent service encounter British abuse policies as evidence of systematic service dysfunction rather than admirable worker protection.

The employment implications of abuse policies include reduced job satisfaction for workers who must implement policies that protect them from customer frustration caused by management decisions beyond their control. Front-line staff become enforcement agents for corporate cost-cutting strategies while bearing the psychological burden of customer complaints about service failures they cannot address.

Staff turnover in customer service roles reflects the unsustainable nature of employment that requires workers to manage customer frustration with systematic service failures. High turnover rates create additional service problems while increasing training costs and reducing service competence, creating negative cycles that abuse policies fail to address.

The democratic implications of abuse policies extend beyond commercial relationships to broader patterns of institutional unaccountability that affect public services and governmental responsiveness. Citizens conditioned to accept business abuse of customer relationships develop lower expectations for public service accountability and institutional responsiveness.

Public services that adopt abuse policies from commercial sectors create additional barriers to citizen participation in democratic processes while protecting institutional incompetence from public criticism. This transfer of corporate abuse tactics to public service undermines democratic accountability while protecting failing institutions from citizen oversight.

The competitive implications of abuse policies include reduced pressure for service improvement that allows inefficient businesses to survive through customer management rather than service excellence. Industries protected by abuse policies avoid innovation and investment that genuine competition would require, reducing economic efficiency and consumer welfare.

The cultural implications of abuse policies include normalization of corporate dominance over individual consumers that reflects broader patterns of institutional authority over citizen welfare. The acceptance of business abuse of customer relationships indicates cultural submission to institutional power that undermines individual agency and social confidence.

Until Britain recognizes abuse policies as symptoms of systematic service failure rather than legitimate worker protection, customer service standards will continue to deteriorate while businesses profit from managing customer frustration rather than preventing it. The choice facing British commerce is between continued exploitation of customer tolerance through abuse policies and genuine investment in service competence that would eliminate most customer complaints. The current system serves corporate interests while degrading consumer welfare and economic efficiency, creating a service economy based on managed conflict rather than mutual benefit.

The great irony of customer service abuse policies is that they protect businesses from accountability for creating the very conditions that generate customer frustration, transforming commercial relationships from mutual exchange into exercises in corporate domination disguised as worker protection. Until British businesses learn to prevent customer frustration through service competence rather than manage it through abuse policies, the service economy will continue to reflect institutional failure rather than commercial excellence.

# Financial Services: The Hollow Crown

The City of London presents itself as a global financial powerhouse, the beating heart of international capitalism where brilliant minds manage vast fortunes through superior expertise and innovative thinking. This mythology conceals a more sordid reality: London's financial dominance rests not on genuine economic excellence but on regulatory arbitrage, tax avoidance schemes, and money laundering services that attract capital fleeing accountability in more transparent jurisdictions. The City operates as a sophisticated cleaning service for global wealth rather than a centre of productive economic activity.

The statistical foundation of London's financial importance reveals its dependence on regulatory weakness rather than economic strength. City of London Economic Data (2024) shows that foreign exchange trading, derivatives markets, and international banking activities concentrate in London primarily because British regulatory authorities permit transactions that other jurisdictions restrict or prohibit. This is not evidence of British financial sophistication but proof that London serves as a haven for capital seeking to avoid oversight and accountability.

The Global Financial Centres Index from Z/Yen Group (2024) consistently ranks London among the top financial centres, but analysis of the criteria reveals that regulatory permissiveness weighs heavily in these rankings alongside traditional measures of economic activity. London competes with jurisdictions like Singapore, Hong Kong, and Switzerland by offering similar services to wealthy individuals and corporations seeking to minimize tax obligations and regulatory compliance.

Brexit has exposed the artificial nature of London's financial supremacy by forcing acknowledgment that much of the City's activity depended on European Union passporting rights that allowed British institutions to serve European clients without meaningful European oversight. Post-Brexit relocations of financial activity to European cities demonstrate that loyalty to London was commercial convenience rather than recognition of superior British financial capabilities.

The exodus of financial institutions following Brexit reveals the mobility of capital that previously appeared to represent British economic strength. Major banks, insurance companies, and asset managers have relocated operations to Frankfurt, Paris, Amsterdam, and Dublin without experiencing significant operational difficulties. This seamless transition proves that London's advantages were regulatory rather than operational, and that financial activity can be relocated quickly when regulatory arbitrage opportunities disappear.

Employment in London's financial sector increasingly depends on foreign talent rather than British expertise, undermining claims about indigenous financial capabilities. International banks staff their London operations with professionals recruited globally rather than trained domestically, while British universities struggle to produce graduates capable of competing in sophisticated financial markets. The City operates as a platform for global talent rather than a showcase for British financial education.

The historical development of London's financial dominance reflects imperial wealth accumulation and currency management rather than innovative financial thinking. The City emerged as a global centre through administration of colonial wealth extraction and sterling currency flows that created artificial demand for

London-based financial services. As empire contracted, London maintained its position by facilitating capital flows that other jurisdictions restricted, particularly during the development of the Eurodollar markets in the 1960s.

The regulatory environment that supports London's financial sector operates through deliberate ambiguity that allows questionable transactions while maintaining plausible deniability about their ultimate purpose. Financial conduct authorities permit complex structures that obscure beneficial ownership, facilitate tax avoidance, and enable money laundering while maintaining that they enforce international standards. This regulatory theatre provides legal cover for activities that would be illegal in more transparent jurisdictions.

The tax haven network that supports London's financial activities operates through British overseas territories and crown dependencies that provide secrecy services while maintaining formal independence from British jurisdiction. The British Virgin Islands, Cayman Islands, Jersey, Guernsey, and other territories offer incorporation services, banking secrecy, and regulatory opacity that complement London's financial offerings. This network allows the City to facilitate tax avoidance while denying direct responsibility for enabling fiscal non-compliance.

Research from the Tax Justice Network (2023) identifies London as the centre of the world's largest tax haven network, facilitating an estimated $21 trillion in offshore wealth held in British territories and dependencies. This massive accumulation of hidden wealth generates fees for London's financial institutions while depriving governments worldwide of tax revenues needed for public services and infrastructure investment.

The money laundering capabilities that attract international capital to London operate through sophisticated legal and financial structures that disguise the origins of questionable wealth. Offshore companies, trust arrangements, and complex ownership structures allow individuals and organizations to move money through London's financial system while obscuring its sources and ultimate destinations. These services attract capital from regions where transparent financial systems would expose corruption and criminal activity.

The property market provides the most visible example of London's role in international money laundering, with residential and commercial real estate serving as vehicles for disguising the proceeds of corruption and criminal activity. Foreign nationals purchase expensive London properties through offshore companies that conceal beneficial ownership, transforming questionable wealth into apparently legitimate assets. This activity inflates property prices while providing cleaning services for international corruption.

Art markets, luxury goods, and other high-value assets traded through London serve similar money laundering functions by converting questionable cash into portable wealth that can be moved internationally without triggering reporting requirements. Auction houses, private banks, and wealth management firms facilitate these transactions while maintaining that they comply with anti-money laundering regulations that are deliberately ineffective.

The private banking sector that serves ultra-high-net-worth individuals operates through secrecy arrangements that prioritize client confidentiality over tax compliance and regulatory transparency. Swiss-style banking secrecy has migrated to London through private banks that offer similar services without the reputational risks associated with traditional tax havens. These institutions manage wealth for clients who require discretion about their financial affairs for reasons that rarely withstand scrutiny.

Wealth management services marketed as sophisticated investment advice often function as tax avoidance consultation that helps wealthy clients minimize obligations to their home jurisdictions. Financial advisors design complex structures that exploit differences between national tax systems while maintaining the appearance of legitimate investment planning. These services generate substantial fees while undermining tax systems that fund public services and social infrastructure.

The derivatives markets that generate enormous trading volumes in London often serve speculation and tax avoidance rather than genuine economic hedging or investment. Complex financial instruments allow participants to create artificial losses, defer tax obligations, and disguise the true nature of investment activities. The opacity and complexity of these markets prevent effective regulation while generating fees for financial intermediaries.

Foreign exchange trading concentrated in London benefits from time zone advantages and network effects, but also from regulatory tolerance for practices that other jurisdictions restrict. Currency speculation that destabilizes developing country economies generates profits for London-based institutions while creating economic havoc in vulnerable regions. This predatory activity continues because British regulators prioritize London's market share over international financial stability.

The Islamic finance sector that London has aggressively courted operates through structures that comply with religious requirements while serving many of the same regulatory arbitrage functions as conventional financial products. Sharia-compliant financing often facilitates transactions that would be prohibited or heavily regulated in secular jurisdictions, allowing London to serve clients from regions where transparent banking would expose questionable activities.

The fintech revolution that London claims to lead often involves technologies that facilitate tax avoidance and regulatory evasion rather than genuine financial innovation. Cryptocurrency exchanges, digital payment systems, and automated trading platforms based in London frequently serve clients seeking to avoid oversight rather than improve financial efficiency. These technologies provide new methods for old practices of wealth concealment and regulatory arbitrage.

The legal services that support London's financial sector operate through attorney-client privilege and professional secrecy arrangements that protect questionable transactions from scrutiny. Magic circle law firms design complex structures that exploit regulatory loopholes while maintaining legal deniability about their ultimate purpose. These legal services are essential to London's financial offerings because they provide protection against accountability for facilitating questionable activities.

Accounting firms that provide services to London's financial sector often facilitate tax avoidance and regulatory evasion through complex accounting treatments that disguise the true nature of financial transactions. Transfer pricing manipulation, profit shifting, and accounting standard arbitrage allow multinational corporations to minimize tax obligations while maintaining the appearance of compliance with reporting requirements.

The insurance and reinsurance markets that operate through London serve similar regulatory arbitrage functions by providing coverage for activities that would be uninsurable in more transparent jurisdictions. Lloyd's of London and other insurance markets facilitate questionable activities by providing financial protection against legal and regulatory risks that transparent insurance markets would not cover.

The pension and investment fund management concentrated in London often serves tax avoidance purposes through structures that exploit differences between national pension regulations. International pension arrangements allow wealthy individuals to defer or avoid tax obligations while maintaining access to their wealth through complex trust and investment structures.

The regulatory capture that enables London's financial sector operates through revolving door employment between regulatory agencies and financial institutions that creates conflicts of interest and prevents effective oversight. Former regulators join financial institutions to exploit their insider knowledge, while financial sector professionals move to regulatory positions where they protect their former employers' interests.

The political influence that protects London's financial sector operates through campaign contributions, lobbying activities, and the promise of employment for politicians who support financial sector interests. The City's political power ensures that regulatory reforms are weakened or delayed while tax haven networks receive protection from international pressure for transparency and accountability.

The international impact of London's financial services includes facilitating corruption in developing countries, enabling tax avoidance by multinational corporations, and providing money laundering services for criminal organizations. These activities generate profits for London's financial institutions while imposing costs on societies worldwide through reduced tax revenues, increased inequality, and weakened governance institutions.

The economic development that London's financial sector claims to promote often involves extractive activities that benefit financial intermediaries while imposing costs on productive economies. Financial engineering that maximizes fees for London-based institutions frequently involves structures that reduce productive investment, increase debt burdens, and create economic instability in client jurisdictions.

The employment that London's financial sector provides often involves facilitating activities that undermine employment and economic development elsewhere. Tax avoidance schemes that reduce government revenues limit public investment in education, infrastructure, and social services that support employment in productive sectors. Money laundering services that protect criminal proceeds undermine rule of law and economic development in affected regions.

The innovation that London's financial sector claims to produce often involves new methods for old practices of wealth extraction and regulatory evasion rather than genuine improvements in financial efficiency or economic productivity. Financial innovation frequently serves rent-seeking activities that transfer wealth from productive sectors to financial intermediaries without creating corresponding economic value.

The competition that London faces from other financial centres reflects the mobility of capital seeking regulatory arbitrage rather than genuine economic advantages. As other jurisdictions develop competitive tax haven networks and money laundering capabilities, London's advantages erode unless British authorities continue to weaken regulatory standards and transparency requirements.

The future sustainability of London's financial sector depends on maintaining regulatory arbitrage opportunities that conflict with international efforts to combat tax avoidance, money laundering, and financial crime. As global pressure for transparency and accountability increases, London must choose between maintaining its current business model and participating in international efforts to improve financial system integrity.

Until Britain acknowledges that London's financial dominance rests on regulatory weakness rather than economic strength, the City will continue to serve questionable capital while undermining international efforts to create transparent and accountable financial systems. The choice facing London is between continued service as a money laundering centre and transformation into a legitimate financial hub that serves productive economic activity rather than wealth concealment and tax avoidance.

The hollow crown of London's financial supremacy reflects the broader pattern of British decline disguised as continued relevance, providing services that sophisticated economies increasingly reject while claiming leadership in activities that undermine global economic development and social justice.

# The Innovation Illusion

British politicians and business leaders never tire of proclaiming Britain as a world-leading innovation hub, the birthplace of the industrial revolution that continues to punch above its weight in scientific discovery and technological advancement. This comfortable mythology allows the nation to avoid confronting the uncomfortable reality that modern Britain has become a consumer of innovation rather than a creator, importing technological solutions developed elsewhere while contributing little to the global knowledge economy beyond historical reputation and inflated self-regard.

The statistical evidence demolishes any legitimate claim to contemporary innovation leadership. R&D Investment Statistics from the OECD (2024) reveal that Britain spends just 1.7% of GDP on research and development, ranking 19th among developed nations and falling well below the OECD average of 2.4%. South Korea invests 4.8% of GDP in R&D, Israel invests 4.9%, while even France and Germany invest substantially more than Britain in proportion to their economic output. This underinvestment reflects political priorities that Favor short-term consumption over long-term innovation capacity.

Patent Filing Data from the UK Intellectual Property Office (2024) shows Britain's declining contribution to global intellectual property creation. British patent applications have stagnated for over a decade while Chinese, American, and even smaller European nations have dramatically increased their innovation output. The patents that Britain does produce increasingly involve incremental improvements to existing technologies rather than breakthrough innovations that create new industries or transform existing ones.

The Global Innovation Index from the World Intellectual Property Organization (2024) places Britain outside the top ten innovative economies, trailing Switzerland, Sweden, Singapore, the United States, Finland, Denmark, South Korea, Germany, and Japan. This ranking reflects comprehensive analysis of innovation inputs, outputs, and efficiency measures that reveal Britain's declining capacity to translate economic resources into innovative outcomes. The gap between British self-perception and international assessment exposes the mythological nature of claims about British innovation leadership.

University research output provides even starker evidence of British innovation decline relative to international competitors. While British universities maintain respectable international rankings, their research increasingly depends on foreign funding, foreign researchers, and collaboration with foreign institutions rather than indigenous innovation capacity. The most productive British researchers are often foreign nationals who could relocate their work elsewhere if British research conditions deteriorate further.

The brain drain affecting British research reflects the superior opportunities available in other innovation economies that invest more heavily in research infrastructure and offer better career prospects for talented researchers. British-trained scientists and engineers emigrate to the United States, Germany, Switzerland, and even emerging economies that provide better research funding and career development opportunities than British institutions can offer.

Government funding for research has declined in real terms over the past decade despite political rhetoric about supporting innovation and building a knowledge economy. The 'Innovation

Gap' study from the CBI (2023) documents systematic underinvestment in research infrastructure, reduced support for early-stage research, and bureaucratic obstacles that discourage private sector research investment. This policy environment reflects political priorities that Favor immediate consumption over long-term innovation capacity.

The historical claims about British innovation leadership rest largely on achievements from the industrial revolution and early twentieth century that have little relevance to contemporary innovation challenges. While Britain did pioneer steam engines, railways, and early telecommunications, these historical achievements do not translate into current innovation capacity any more than ancient Greek mathematics makes modern Greece a technology leader.

The myth of continuing British innovation excellence relies heavily on selective citation of individual success stories while ignoring systematic patterns of innovation decline and international comparison data. Occasional British successes in pharmaceuticals, aerospace, or digital technology are highlighted while systematic underperformance across most innovation sectors receives minimal attention. This cherry-picking creates false impressions about overall British innovation performance.

The pharmaceutical industry provides the most commonly cited evidence of British innovation leadership, yet analysis reveals heavy dependence on foreign ownership, foreign research funding, and international collaboration rather than indigenous British innovation capacity. Major pharmaceutical companies operating in Britain are primarily foreign-owned entities that could relocate their research activities to other countries if British conditions become less attractive.

AstraZeneca, often cited as a British pharmaceutical success story, results from merger between British and Swedish companies and operates internationally rather than as specifically British enterprise. The company's research activities are distributed globally, with significant operations in the United States, Sweden, and other countries that offer competitive research environments. Claims about British pharmaceutical innovation often conflate international companies' British operations with indigenous British innovation capacity.

The aerospace industry represents another area where claims about British innovation exceed the reality of contemporary British contributions to technological advancement. While Britain maintains involvement in international aerospace projects, these typically involve junior partnership roles in American or European programs rather than British leadership in innovative aerospace development.

Rolls-Royce aerospace engines are frequently cited as evidence of British technological excellence, yet the company's success depends heavily on international collaboration, foreign components, and global supply chains rather than uniquely British technological capabilities. The engines represent sophisticated engineering rather than breakthrough innovation, and similar capabilities exist in other countries with comparable industrial development.

The digital technology sector reveals perhaps the starkest gap between British innovation mythology and contemporary reality. While London has developed a significant financial technology cluster, most "British" fintech innovation involves application of technologies developed elsewhere rather than fundamental technological breakthroughs originating in Britain. The sector succeeds through regulatory arbitrage and financial sector connections rather than technological innovation.

British technology companies that achieve international success typically involve business model innovation rather than technological innovation, adapting technologies developed elsewhere to serve specific market niches. This commercial success, while economically valuable, does not constitute the technological innovation that creates new industries or transforms existing technological paradigms.

The artificial intelligence sector provides clear evidence of British innovation decline relative to international competitors. While Britain hosts some AI research activities, the leading AI companies, research institutions, and technological breakthroughs originate in the United States, China, and increasingly in smaller countries that invest more heavily in AI research and development. British AI activities typically involve application of technologies developed elsewhere rather than fundamental AI innovation.

The quantum computing field, often cited as an area of British strength, actually demonstrates the gap between British research capabilities and the resources required for technological leadership. While British universities conduct quantum research, the massive investments required for quantum computing development occur primarily in the United States, China, and Germany. British quantum research remains largely academic rather than commercially oriented.

The renewable energy sector reveals similar patterns of British underperformance in innovation despite political rhetoric about green technology leadership. Wind turbine technology develops primarily in Denmark and Germany, solar technology advances primarily in China and the United States, while battery technology develops primarily in Asian countries that invest heavily in energy storage research. British renewable energy activities typically involve deployment of technologies developed elsewhere rather than innovation in green technology.

The automotive industry provides stark evidence of British innovation decline, with British car manufacturing now consisting primarily of foreign-owned assembly operations rather than innovative automotive development. The internal combustion engine technology that Britain pioneered has been superseded by electric vehicle technology developed primarily in the United States, China, and Germany. British automotive activities increasingly involve manufacturing components designed elsewhere rather than automotive innovation.

The space industry represents another area where British claims about innovation exceed contemporary British contributions to space technology development. While Britain participates in European Space Agency programs and hosts some commercial space activities, the major space technology innovations occur in the United States, China, and increasingly in private companies that operate internationally rather than as specifically British enterprises.

The biotechnology sector demonstrates the limitations of British innovation capacity despite significant university research activities. While British universities conduct important biological research, the translation of research into commercial biotechnology products typically requires investment levels and market access that British companies struggle to achieve. Successful British biotechnology research often gets acquired by foreign companies that possess the resources necessary for commercial development.

The materials science field reveals similar patterns of British research strength but commercial weakness, with innovative materials developed in British universities often commercialized by foreign companies that possess superior manufacturing capabilities and market access. This pattern reflects the systematic British weakness in translating research into commercial innovation rather than fundamental research incapacity.

The telecommunications sector provides evidence of British decline from early leadership to current dependence on foreign technology suppliers. While Britain pioneered early telecommunications technology, contemporary telecommunications infrastructure depends heavily on equipment from Chinese, American, and European suppliers rather than British technology companies. The 5G telecommunications deployment in Britain involves foreign technology rather than British innovation.

The semiconductor industry reveals the most dramatic evidence of British innovation decline, with Britain having essentially no domestic semiconductor manufacturing capability despite the critical importance of semiconductors for all modern technology. British technology companies depend entirely on foreign semiconductor suppliers, making Britain vulnerable to supply chain disruptions and technological dependence on other countries.

The software development sector shows mixed British performance, with strengths in specific applications but limited contribution to fundamental software innovation that creates new technological paradigms. British software companies typically focus on business applications rather than the systems software, artificial intelligence, or advanced computing technologies that drive technological transformation.

The research infrastructure that supports innovation has deteriorated in Britain due to chronic underinvestment in laboratory facilities, research equipment, and technical support staff. British universities struggle to maintain research capabilities that match international standards, while government research institutions face budget constraints that limit their contribution to innovation development.

The education system that should produce innovative researchers and engineers has failed to adapt to contemporary innovation requirements, with science and engineering education that emphasizes traditional subjects rather than emerging technologies. British universities produce fewer engineering and computer science graduates than economic competitors, while the quality of technical education has declined relative to international standards.

The immigration policies that could attract international talent to British innovation activities have become increasingly restrictive, making it difficult for British institutions to recruit the foreign researchers and engineers necessary for competitive innovation programs. Brexit has particularly damaged Britain's ability to participate in European research collaboration and attract European research talent.

The venture capital and private equity sectors that should support innovation commercialization remain underdeveloped in Britain compared to the United States and increasingly compared to Asian innovation economies. British investors typically focus on property and financial services rather than technology investment, while the scale of British technology investment remains inadequate for developing major innovation companies.

The procurement policies that could support British innovation development instead Favor foreign suppliers and established technologies rather than encouraging domestic innovation development. Government procurement rarely supports innovative British companies, while defence and infrastructure spending typically involves foreign technology rather than British innovation development.

The regulatory environment that should encourage innovation often creates obstacles to technology development and commercialization, with complex approval processes and risk-averse regulatory approaches that discourage innovative activities. The contrast with innovation-friendly regulatory environments in other countries makes Britain less attractive for innovation development and commercialization.

The cultural attitudes toward risk and entrepreneurship in Britain remain conservative compared to innovation economies that celebrate technological risk-taking and accept innovation failures as learning opportunities. British business culture emphasizes financial engineering and short-term returns rather than long-term technology development, while British society remains sceptical of technological change and entrepreneurial success.

The international collaboration that modern innovation requires has become more difficult for Britain due to Brexit and declining international research relationships. Innovation increasingly requires international partnerships and global research networks that Britain finds harder to access as its international standing and research attractiveness decline.

Until Britain acknowledges that innovation leadership requires sustained investment, systematic policy support, and long-term commitment rather than historical reputation and political rhetoric, the nation will continue to decline in global innovation rankings while depending increasingly on technologies developed elsewhere. The choice facing Britain is between honest assessment of innovation weaknesses and continued investment in innovation mythology that prevents the systematic changes necessary for genuine innovation development.

The innovation illusion serves political and psychological needs by maintaining the fiction of British technological leadership while avoiding the difficult decisions and substantial investments required for genuine innovation capacity. This comfortable mythology will persist until external competitive pressure forces acknowledgment that innovation cannot be sustained through reputation alone but requires the same systematic investment and policy commitment that other innovation economies have made to achieve technological leadership.

# Housing: The Speculation Economy

The British housing market represents the transformation of a basic human need into a speculative casino where participants gamble with shelter while congratulating themselves on economic sophistication. This perversion of housing policy has created a property-obsessed culture that treats rising house prices as economic success while condemning entire generations to rental serfdom or permanent exclusion from homeownership. The housing crisis is not an accident of market forces but the deliberate result of policies designed to enrich existing property owners at the expense of everyone else.

The statistics reveal the scale of this manufactured crisis with devastating clarity. House Price Data from the ONS (2024) shows that average house prices have increased by over 400% since 1995, while average wages have increased by only 80% over the same period. This divergence makes homeownership mathematically impossible for most young people without parental assistance, transforming property ownership from reward for work into inheritance privilege. The median house price now exceeds ten times median income in many areas, compared to three times median income in the 1970s.

Home Ownership Statistics from the Department for Levelling Up (2024) reveal that homeownership rates have declined from 71% in 2003 to 63% in 2024, with particularly dramatic declines among people under 35. Young adults who could expect to own homes by their late twenties in previous generations now face average ages of first-time purchase extending into their late thirties, assuming they can purchase at all. This delay represents not personal failure but systematic exclusion from property ownership through deliberate policy choices.

International Housing Affordability data from Dermographia (2024) places British cities among the least affordable in the developed world, with London ranking as the third least affordable major city globally after Hong Kong and Sydney. This comparison exposes the artificial nature of British housing costs, as countries with similar population densities and land constraints achieve much more affordable housing through different policy approaches. British housing costs reflect policy choices rather than geographical inevitability.

The rental market has become a wealth extraction mechanism that transfers money from working people to property-owning landlords while providing minimal security or quality for tenants. Average rental costs consume over 40% of median income in most British cities, compared to 25% in Germany and 30% in France. This rental burden prevents tenants from saving for house deposits while enriching landlords who often acquired their properties through inheritance or family assistance rather than earned income.

The geography of housing inequality reinforces broader patterns of regional and generational disadvantage while concentrating opportunity in areas where housing costs exclude working-class participation. London and the South East offer the highest salaries and best career prospects, but housing costs ensure that these opportunities remain available primarily to those whose families can provide financial support. Regional house price variations create internal migration pressures that separate families and communities while concentrating wealth in expensive areas.

The generational impact of housing speculation has created unprecedented wealth transfers from young to old that undermine social cohesion and democratic legitimacy. Property owners who purchased homes when they were affordable have benefited from unearned capital gains that exceed most people's lifetime earnings, while younger generations face housing costs that consume the majority of their income throughout their working lives. This wealth transfer occurs without corresponding productivity increases or economic contribution from property owners.

The role of inheritance in determining housing access reveals the restoration of hereditary advantage through property wealth that makes a mockery of meritocratic principles. According to 'The Housing Crisis' study from Shelter (2024), over 60% of first-time buyers now receive family assistance for deposits, while those without family wealth remain excluded from property ownership indefinitely. This dependence on inheritance transforms housing from reward for work into marker of family privilege.

Property speculation by existing homeowners has distorted the housing market through buy-to-let investments that extract rental income while inflating house prices beyond the reach of potential owner-occupiers. Landlords compete with first-time buyers for the same properties while enjoying tax advantages and capital appreciation that make rental investment more profitable than productive economic activity. This speculation diverts capital from productive investment toward rent-seeking activities that create no economic value.

Foreign investment in British property provides additional speculative pressure that drives house prices beyond any relationship to local incomes or housing demand. Wealthy individuals and sovereign wealth funds purchase British properties as investments rather than homes, treating British housing as a commodity in global wealth portfolios. This financialization of housing ensures that property prices reflect international capital flows rather than domestic housing needs.

The planning system operates as a supply restriction mechanism that artificially constrains housing development to protect existing property values while claiming environmental and community protection motives. Local authorities dominated by existing homeowners consistently oppose housing development that would increase supply and reduce property values, using planning regulations to prevent construction that would make housing more affordable. This democratic capture ensures that housing policy serves existing property owners rather than housing need.

Green belt policies that prevent housing development near cities force longer commutes, higher transport costs, and greater environmental impact while protecting property values for existing homeowners. The green belt operates as a exclusion zone that concentrates development pressure in areas where existing residents lack political power to resist, creating environmental and social problems while preserving rural amenity for wealthy property owners.

Building regulations and construction standards that appear to protect quality and safety often serve to increase construction costs and complexity while creating barriers to affordable housing development. The regulatory framework favours large construction companies that can navigate complex approval processes while excluding smaller developers who might provide more affordable housing alternatives. This regulatory capture ensures that new housing serves high-end markets rather than addressing broader housing need.

The construction industry has evolved into an oligopoly of large companies that prioritize profit margins over housing supply, building expensive homes for affluent buyers rather than affordable housing for working families. These companies deliberately restrict supply to maintain high prices while claiming that land costs, regulations, and planning delays prevent them from building more affordable housing. The industry's business model depends on housing scarcity rather than housing abundance.

Social housing provision has been systematically dismantled through right-to-buy policies that transferred public assets to private ownership while failing to replace sold properties with new social housing. The reduction in social housing stock forces working families into private rental markets where they face higher costs and reduced security while enriching private landlords. This privatization of social housing represents one of the largest transfers of public wealth to private hands in British history.

Housing associations that replaced local authority housing provision operate as quasi-private entities that prioritize financial sustainability over social housing mission, developing expensive market-rate housing while providing minimal affordable housing. These organizations exploit public subsidy and charitable status while behaving like private developers, contributing to housing speculation rather than providing affordable alternatives to market housing.

The mortgage market operates through lending criteria that exclude working-class buyers while facilitating speculative investment by existing property owners who can leverage equity from previous property appreciation. Banks readily lend to landlords purchasing additional properties while applying strict affordability criteria to first-time buyers, ensuring that property ownership concentrates among those who already possess property wealth.

Interest rate policies that claim to control inflation consistently prioritize asset price protection over housing affordability, keeping interest rates low to protect existing property owners from negative equity while ensuring that house prices remain unaffordable for new buyers. The Bank of England's monetary policy serves property speculation rather than economic stability or social welfare.

Tax policies provide systematic advantages to property speculation while penalizing productive economic activity, treating capital gains from property appreciation more favourably than earnings from work. Property investors benefit from mortgage interest relief, capital gains deferrals, and inheritance tax advantages that are unavailable to people who work for their income. This tax system encourages speculation while discouraging productive investment.

Council tax based on 1991 property valuations creates regressive taxation that undercharges expensive properties while overcharging modest homes, subsidizing wealthy property owners while burdening working families. The failure to update property valuations for over thirty years represents deliberate policy choice to protect wealthy property owners from paying their fair share of local taxation.

Stamp duty designed to discourage property speculation instead creates market distortions that reduce housing mobility while failing to prevent speculative investment. The tax structure encourages property hoarding by existing owners while creating barriers to housing transactions that reduce market efficiency. This poorly designed taxation fails to address housing speculation while creating additional obstacles to housing access.

The cultural obsession with property ownership treats housing as investment rather than shelter, encouraging speculative behaviour that inflates property values while treating housing as commodity rather than human right. Television programs celebrate property development and speculation while ignoring the social costs of housing unaffordability. This cultural reinforcement of property speculation normalizes housing inequality while treating affordable housing as threat to property values.

Property television programming promotes speculation by presenting property investment as accessible wealth creation strategy while ignoring the mathematical impossibility of universal property speculation. These programs encourage viewers to participate in housing speculation without acknowledging that speculation profits depend on excluding others from property ownership. The entertainment industry promotes property speculation while concealing its social costs.

Regional development policies that claim to address housing inequality often exacerbate regional disparities by concentrating investment in areas where housing is already expensive while neglecting areas where housing remains affordable. Government investment in transport, education, and economic development increases property values in target areas while failing to create housing supply that would make development benefits accessible to working families.

Urban regeneration projects consistently involve displacement of existing communities through gentrification that replaces affordable housing with expensive developments marketed to affluent newcomers. These projects receive public subsidy while serving private property speculation, destroying communities while enriching developers and property investors. The pattern repeats across British cities with predictable results that policymakers refuse to acknowledge.

The economic impact of housing speculation includes reduced labour mobility, decreased entrepreneurship, and lower productivity as workers cannot relocate to areas with better opportunities due to housing costs. Regional economic development suffers when businesses cannot recruit workers who cannot afford local housing, while economic dynamism declines when workers cannot move to areas where their skills would be most productive.

Innovation and entrepreneurship suffer when potential entrepreneurs cannot access affordable housing that would allow them to take risks with new business ventures. High housing costs force people into employment that provides housing security rather than pursuing innovative activities that might fail initially but could generate greater long-term economic value.

Consumer spending patterns distorted by high housing costs reduce demand for goods and services that would support broader economic activity, as families spend larger proportions of income on housing rather than consumption that would support employment in other sectors. This distortion reduces economic multiplier effects while concentrating wealth in property markets.

The social consequences of housing speculation include delayed family formation, reduced birth rates, and weakened community cohesion as people cannot afford to live near their families or remain in communities where they grew up. These social costs affect future economic productivity and social stability while enriching current property owners.

Mental health impacts of housing insecurity include increased anxiety, depression, and social isolation among people who cannot achieve housing stability or homeownership despite working consistently and earning reasonable incomes. The psychological stress of housing insecurity affects work performance and social relationships while creating healthcare costs that society bears collectively.

Democratic consequences of housing speculation include reduced political participation among renters who move frequently and cannot develop community connections, while homeowners vote to protect property values rather than broader social welfare. This political distortion ensures that housing policy continues to serve property speculation rather than housing need.

Until Britain acknowledges that housing speculation serves existing property owners at the expense of broader social welfare, housing policy will continue to prioritize property values over housing affordability and social cohesion. The choice facing Britain is between continued housing speculation that enriches property owners while excluding others from homeownership, and housing policies that prioritize shelter provision over investment returns. The current system serves property speculation rather than housing need, creating social division and economic inefficiency that will persist until housing policy serves human welfare rather than property wealth.

The speculation economy has transformed housing from basic need into investment commodity, creating artificial scarcity that enriches existing property owners while imposing social costs that undermine economic dynamism and social cohesion. This transformation reflects policy choices rather than market inevitability, and can be reversed through policies that prioritize housing provision over property speculation.

# Imperial Nostalgia: The Phantom Empire

British foreign policy operates as an elaborate exercise in imperial cosplay, with politicians, diplomats, and military leaders acting out roles from a global empire that ended decades ago while pretending that ceremony and tradition compensate for the loss of actual power and influence. This pathetic nostalgia for imperial grandeur prevents honest assessment of Britain's diminished international position while encouraging delusional policies based on fantasies about British global importance that exist nowhere outside the British imagination.

The statistical reality of British international influence demolishes any legitimate claim to continued global leadership. Commonwealth Trade Statistics from the Commonwealth Secretariat (2024) reveal that Britain accounts for less than 15% of total Commonwealth trade, while intra-Commonwealth trade represents only 9% of total Commonwealth economic activity. Former British colonies conduct the overwhelming majority of their international commerce with countries other than Britain, demonstrating their successful transition to independent economic relationships that do not require British involvement.

Economic data from the World Bank (2024) shows that India's economy is now larger than Britain's, while Australia, Canada, and South Africa conduct most of their trade with Asian and American partners rather than their former colonial metropole. These Commonwealth countries have developed into mature economies that relate to Britain as one trading partner among many rather than as dependent territories requiring British guidance or leadership. India's GDP reached $3.7 trillion in 2024, surpassing Britain's $3.1 trillion, while conducting only 1.2% of its total trade with its former colonial ruler.

Military cooperation statistics reveal the hollow nature of Commonwealth defence relationships, with former British colonies maintaining minimal defence cooperation with Britain while developing extensive military partnerships with regional powers and global superpowers. Australia's AUKUS partnership explicitly excludes Britain from key technology transfers, while Canada integrates its defence planning with the United States rather than Britain. Even countries that maintain ceremonial ties to the British monarchy pursue defence policies independent of British strategic planning.

The persistence of the Commonwealth as institutional framework provides convenient fiction for British politicians seeking to maintain illusions about global influence, but analysis of Commonwealth summits and initiatives reveals their irrelevance to contemporary international relations. Commonwealth declarations receive minimal international attention while achieving no practical results, as member countries pursue national interests through more effective international organizations and bilateral relationships. The 2022 Commonwealth Heads of Government Meeting in Rwanda produced 19 separate declarations and commitments that have resulted in virtually no measurable policy changes or international cooperation.

Royal visits to Commonwealth countries generate ceremonial coverage that creates false impressions about British influence while highlighting the anachronistic nature of constitutional monarchies in independent nations. The pageantry of royal tours conceals the reality that host countries tolerate these visits as historical curiosities rather than meaningful diplomatic engagements. The cost and complexity of royal security arrangements often exceed any diplomatic benefits these visits might theoretically provide. The 2022 Caribbean royal tour faced protests in several countries and calls for reparations rather than the warm reception that British media anticipated.

Cultural influence through the Commonwealth represents another area where British assumptions about soft power exceed the reality of contemporary cultural flows. English language usage owes more to American economic and cultural dominance than to British imperial history, while Commonwealth countries develop independent cultural identities that increasingly diverge from British cultural influences. British cultural exports to Commonwealth countries compete unsuccessfully with American, Asian, and indigenous cultural products. Bollywood films grossed $2.4 billion globally in 2023, while British films struggled to find audiences even in former British colonies.

Educational relationships through Commonwealth universities and student exchanges operate on much smaller scales than British rhetoric suggests, while Commonwealth students increasingly choose American, Canadian, and Australian universities over British institutions. The brain drain from Commonwealth countries to Britain has reversed in many cases, with British graduates seeking opportunities in dynamic Commonwealth economies rather than remaining in economically stagnant Britain. Australian universities now attract more international students than all British universities combined, while charging lower fees and providing better post-graduation employment opportunities.

The immigration patterns that once reflected imperial relationships have fundamentally changed, with Commonwealth citizens no longer enjoying preferential access to British residence or employment. Brexit immigration policies treat Commonwealth citizens less favourably than European Union citizens were treated, destroying one of the few remaining practical benefits of Commonwealth membership. This immigration policy shift reflects British recognition that Commonwealth relationships provide minimal economic or political advantages. The points-based immigration system introduced in 2021 eliminated preferential treatment for Commonwealth citizens while making it more difficult for skilled workers from former colonies to obtain British work permits.

Post-colonial economic relationships reveal the exploitative nature of imperial nostalgia that treats former colonies as markets for British exports rather than independent economies pursuing their own development strategies. British trade promotion through Commonwealth channels often involves attempting to maintain dependent relationships that Commonwealth countries have successfully transcended through economic diversification and regional integration. Britain's share of Indian imports has declined from 3.2% in 2000 to 0.9% in 2024, while China's share increased from 3.5% to 15.7% over the same period.

The historical revisionism that accompanies imperial nostalgia presents British colonial rule as beneficial modernization rather than extractive exploitation, ignoring extensive scholarship documenting the economic, social, and cultural damage that British colonialism inflicted on subject populations. This sanitized version of imperial history serves contemporary political needs while insulting former colonial subjects who experienced British rule as oppression rather than benevolence. The 2019 YouGov poll revealing that 32% of British respondents thought the British

Empire was "something to be proud of" demonstrates the persistent denial about colonial reality.

Colonial Impact Studies from various academic sources between 2020-2024 demonstrate the systematic extraction of wealth from colonial territories to Britain, the destruction of indigenous economic systems, and the creation of dependent economic relationships that persisted long after formal independence. The economic development that Britain claims to have brought to colonial territories primarily served British interests while impoverishing local populations and distorting economic development toward export of raw materials to Britain. Economic historian Utsa Patnaik's research indicates that Britain extracted approximately $45 trillion from India between 1765 and 1938, representing the largest wealth transfer in human history.

The railway systems that British colonial apologists cite as evidence of beneficial development were designed to extract raw materials to British ports rather than serve indigenous transportation needs, creating transport networks that served colonial extraction rather than local economic development. These railway lines connected resource extraction areas to export ports while failing to connect major population centres or facilitate internal trade. Post-independence governments have spent decades rebuilding transport infrastructure to serve national rather than colonial economic objectives.

Educational systems imposed during colonial rule prioritized producing compliant administrators for colonial bureaucracy rather than developing indigenous knowledge systems or technical capabilities that would support independent economic development. Colonial education deliberately suppressed local languages, cultural knowledge, and technical traditions while producing graduates dependent on British institutional frameworks. The legacy of colonial education systems continues to affect post-colonial development decades after independence.

The partition of India provides the starkest example of British imperial legacy creating ongoing conflict and instability rather than beneficial development. British departure from India involved hasty partition that created refugee crises, communal violence, and permanent territorial disputes between India and Pakistan. The Kashmir conflict, Indo-Pakistani wars, and regional instability that continues today reflect British failure to manage decolonization responsibly rather than evidence of British administrative competence.

## Case Study 1: Kashmir - The Unfinished Partition

The Kashmir conflict represents the most enduring and dangerous legacy of British imperial mismanagement, creating a territorial dispute that has generated four wars, continuous military tension, and the threat of nuclear conflict between India and Pakistan. British colonial authorities created this crisis through deliberate ambiguity about princely state accession procedures and hasty departure that left fundamental constitutional questions unresolved.

The 1947 partition plan developed by British officials failed to establish clear procedures for princely state accession to either India or Pakistan, creating legal ambiguity that British authorities used to avoid responsibility for difficult decisions about territorial boundaries. Kashmir, as a Muslim-majority state ruled by a Hindu maharaja, represented the most complex case that British officials deliberately left unresolved rather than making decisions that might complicate British departure from the subcontinent.

When Pakistani tribal forces invaded Kashmir in October 1947, British officials refused to provide guidance about legal procedures for Indian military intervention or Pakistani territorial claims, forcing newly independent governments to make crucial decisions about sovereignty and territorial integrity without clear legal framework. This British abdication of responsibility created the conditions for military conflict that has continued for over seven decades.

The ceasefire line established in 1949 through United Nations mediation created temporary boundaries that became permanent division without resolution of underlying sovereignty questions. British representatives in the UN Security Council supported resolutions calling for plebiscites that they knew were impractical while avoiding any commitment to facilitate actual conflict resolution. This pattern of supporting unrealistic solutions while avoiding practical responsibility has characterized British policy toward Kashmir throughout the conflict.

The Line of Control that divides Kashmir has become one of the world's most militarized borders, with over 500,000 Indian and Pakistani troops deployed in the region at enormous economic and human cost. The military expenditure required to maintain this deployment diverts resources from development projects that could improve living standards in both countries, while creating permanent military tension that prevents regional economic cooperation.

Kashmiris themselves have borne the human cost of this British-created conflict through decades of military occupation, political violence, and economic underdevelopment that result from territorial uncertainty. The disputed status prevents normal economic development while subjecting civilian populations to military rule and human rights violations that would be unacceptable in undisputed territories.

The nuclear dimension added to the Kashmir conflict in 1998 transformed a regional territorial dispute into a global security threat that could trigger nuclear war between India and Pakistan. The Kargil conflict of 1999 and the 2019 Balakot airstrikes demonstrated how easily Kashmir tensions can escalate to military action between nuclear-armed states. This escalation potential makes the Kashmir conflict one of the world's most dangerous flashpoints.

British governments consistently avoid acknowledging their responsibility for creating the Kashmir conflict while offering symbolic mediation services that serve no practical purpose beyond maintaining the fiction of British diplomatic relevance. These mediation offers are rejected by both India and Pakistan, which recognize that Britain lacks the influence or impartiality necessary for effective conflict resolution.

The economic cost of the Kashmir conflict includes not only direct military expenditure but also the opportunity cost of forgone regional economic integration that could benefit all South Asian countries. Trade between India and Pakistan remains minimal partly due to Kashmir tensions, while regional infrastructure projects that could connect Central Asian and South Asian economies remain impossible due to territorial disputes.

## Case Study 2: Nigeria - The Artificial State and Boko Haram

Nigeria's contemporary security crisis reflects another catastrophic legacy of British colonial boundary-drawing that created artificial states combining incompatible ethnic, religious, and cultural groups without developing institutions capable of managing resulting conflicts. The Boko Haram insurgency that has killed over 35,000 people since 2009 represents the violent culmination of tensions created by British colonial administrative decisions that prioritized administrative convenience over ethnic and religious compatibility.

British colonial authorities combined the northern Hausa-Fulani Muslim emirates with southern Yoruba and Igbo Christian and animist territories to create Nigeria as a single colony, despite these groups having distinct languages, religions, political systems, and economic structures. This amalgamation served British administrative efficiency and economic extraction rather than indigenous political logic or social cohesion.

The indirect rule system that Britain employed in northern Nigeria preserved Islamic governmental structures while imposing Western administrative systems in southern regions, creating incompatible governance models within a single colony. This dual system prevented development of unified national institutions while maintaining religious and cultural divisions that British authorities found useful for colonial control.

Educational policies during colonial rule deliberately maintained different systems in northern and southern Nigeria, with Islamic education continuing in the north while Western missionary education developed in the south. This educational divide created different elite classes with incompatible worldviews and prepared them for different roles in colonial administration rather than integrated national leadership.

The economic development that occurred during colonial rule concentrated modern infrastructure and industry in southern regions while maintaining northern areas as sources of agricultural raw materials and cheap labour. This economic imbalance created regional disparities that persist today, with northern Nigeria remaining significantly poorer and less developed than southern regions.

Independence in 1960 transferred power to indigenous elites who inherited these colonial divisions without institutional mechanisms for managing resulting conflicts. The parliamentary system imposed by British authorities proved incapable of accommodating ethnic and religious diversity, leading to political crises that culminated in civil war between 1967 and 1970.

The Biafran War that killed over one million people resulted directly from ethnic tensions created by British colonial boundary-drawing and administrative policies that favoured some groups over others. British support for the federal government during this conflict reflected concern about oil revenues rather than principled commitment to Nigerian unity or human rights.

Post-independence military governments attempted to manage ethnic and religious tensions through authoritarian control rather than democratic accommodation, creating cycles of military rule and civilian government that prevented development of stable democratic institutions. The weakness of Nigerian democratic institutions reflects colonial legacies that British authorities failed to address during decolonization.

The discovery of oil in southern Nigeria created additional tensions by concentrating wealth in regions that had suffered during colonial rule while providing minimal benefits to northern populations that supplied agricultural products and labour. Oil revenues corrupted Nigerian politics while exacerbating regional inequalities that colonial rule had created.

Boko Haram emerged in northern Nigeria as violent response to decades of political marginalization, economic underdevelopment, and cultural alienation that reflect colonial legacies rather than purely religious extremism. The group's rejection of Western education reflects the colonial association of Western education with southern Christian dominance and northern Muslim subordination.

The insurgency has displaced over 2.3 million people while destroying infrastructure and economic development in northeastern Nigeria, creating humanitarian crisis that affects neighbouring Chad, Cameroon, and Niger. The regional impact reflects the artificial nature of colonial boundaries that divided ethnic groups across multiple countries without regard for social or economic integration.

International military intervention to combat Boko Haram involves France, the United States, and regional African forces rather than Britain, demonstrating that former colonial powers are not necessarily best positioned to address conflicts their colonial policies created. British military assistance to Nigeria remains minimal compared to other international actors who have greater strategic interests in regional stability.

The counter-insurgency strategies employed by Nigerian security forces often involve human rights violations against civilian populations suspected of supporting Boko Haram, creating additional grievances that fuel continued conflict. These heavy-handed military approaches reflect colonial-era policing methods that prioritized control over consent.

African decolonization followed similar patterns of British abandonment creating instability and conflict rather than smooth transition to independence. British colonial authorities failed to develop indigenous administrative capacity, created artificial boundaries that ignored ethnic and cultural divisions, and departed without ensuring functional governance structures. The political instability that affected many former British African colonies reflects British colonial mismanagement rather than indigenous incapacity for self-governance.

Middle Eastern boundaries drawn by British colonial administrators created artificial states that have generated conflict and instability throughout the region. Iraq, created by combining disparate Ottoman provinces, has experienced continuous internal conflict since British mandate administration. Palestine partition created permanent refugee populations and ongoing conflict that British policy helped create but failed to resolve.

The Balfour Declaration of 1917 promised Jewish national homeland in Palestine while guaranteeing that "nothing shall be done which may prejudice the civil and religious rights of existing non-Jewish communities in Palestine." British authorities proved incapable of reconciling these incompatible commitments, creating permanent conflict that continues to destabilize the Middle East while providing no practical benefits to any parties involved.

The mandate system that Britain administered in Iraq, Palestine, and other Middle Eastern territories served British strategic interests rather than local political development, creating dependent relationships that prevented indigenous institutional development. British departure from these territories left power vacuums that generated ongoing conflict rather than stable independent governments.

The Suez Crisis of 1956 marked the definitive end of British imperial power when American pressure forced British withdrawal from military action designed to maintain imperial influence in the Middle East. This humiliation demonstrated that Britain could no longer act independently in pursuit of imperial interests when American policy opposed British actions. The crisis should have ended imperial nostalgia, but instead generated defensive mythologies about American betrayal of British interests.

The Falklands War of 1982 provided temporary revival of imperial mythology through military success against Argentina, but analysis reveals that British victory depended on American logistical support and Argentine military incompetence rather than superior British military capabilities. The conflict involved colonial territory that serves no strategic purpose beyond symbolic assertion of British territorial claims, making military expenditure for Falklands defence economically irrational.

The continued possession of overseas territories like Gibraltar, the Falklands, and various Caribbean islands serves no practical British interests while creating diplomatic complications and defence expenditures that exceed any conceivable benefits. These territorial claims reflect imperial nostalgia rather than strategic calculation, maintaining symbolic presence at real cost to British resources and international relationships.

Gibraltar's status creates ongoing diplomatic tension with Spain that complicates British relationships with European Union neighbours while providing no strategic benefits that justify the political costs. The territory's economy depends on financial services that operate through regulatory arbitrage rather than productive economic activity, making Gibraltar another tax haven that serves international capital rather than British strategic interests.

Naval deployment policies that maintain British warships in distant waters serve ceremonial rather than strategic purposes, projecting images of global reach while contributing nothing to actual British security or economic interests. These deployments consume defence resources while providing no meaningful military capabilities that could not be better employed in European or North Atlantic contexts where British security interests actually exist.

The Queen Elizabeth-class aircraft carriers represent the pinnacle of imperial nostalgia, costing over £6 billion while serving no strategic purpose that justifies their enormous expense. These ships operate American aircraft under American logistical support while projecting British presence in regions where Britain has no vital interests to defend. The carriers serve symbolic rather than strategic functions while consuming resources that could address genuine security challenges.

Defence relationships with former colonies often involve British weapons sales rather than genuine security cooperation, using historical relationships to promote British defence exports rather than providing effective security assistance. These commercial relationships disguise arms sales as security cooperation while former colonies increasingly purchase military equipment from other suppliers offering better technology and more favourable terms.

British defence exports to Saudi Arabia and other authoritarian regimes demonstrate how imperial relationships facilitate arms sales that support human rights violations rather than legitimate security needs. The war in Yemen involves British weapons used against civilian targets while generating profits for British defence contractors and maintaining fiction of strategic partnership with former colonial territories.

Intelligence relationships through Five Eyes and other arrangements position Britain as junior partner to American intelligence agencies rather than independent intelligence power, while former colonies develop independent intelligence capabilities that reduce dependence on British intelligence sharing. British intelligence services provide more intelligence to American partners than they receive in return, reflecting asymmetrical relationships that serve American rather than British interests.

The Five Eyes alliance includes Australia, Canada, and New Zealand as equal partners rather than British dependencies, while these countries increasingly develop independent intelligence relationships with Asian and regional partners. British intelligence influence within Five Eyes has declined as other members pursue intelligence cooperation that serves their regional rather than British strategic priorities.

Diplomatic initiatives that attempt to leverage Commonwealth relationships for international influence consistently fail because Commonwealth countries pursue independent foreign policies that often conflict with British positions. Britain cannot deliver

Commonwealth support for international initiatives because it lacks influence over Commonwealth foreign policies, making Commonwealth diplomatic coordination ineffective for advancing British international objectives.

The 2021 withdrawal from Afghanistan proceeded without meaningful consultation with Commonwealth partners despite decades of Commonwealth military contributions to NATO operations in Afghanistan. This exclusion from strategic decision-making demonstrates that Britain cannot leverage Commonwealth relationships for influence over American strategic planning, while Commonwealth countries pursue their own relationships with major powers rather than coordinating through British leadership.

Climate change policies that Britain promotes through Commonwealth channels often conflict with the development priorities of Commonwealth countries that prioritize economic growth over environmental protection. British environmental advocacy appears as attempt to prevent developing Commonwealth countries from achieving the industrial development that Britain used to build its own wealth, creating resentment rather than cooperation.

The COP26 climate summit hosted by Britain in Glasgow failed to achieve meaningful commitments from major Commonwealth countries including India and Australia, demonstrating that historical relationships provide no leverage over contemporary policy decisions. Commonwealth countries coordinate climate policies through regional organizations and bilateral relationships rather than through British-led initiatives.

Trade promotion through Commonwealth channels faces competition from more attractive trading relationships that

Commonwealth countries maintain with regional partners and global economic powers. British exports to Commonwealth countries face the same competitive pressures as exports to other countries, while Britain cannot offer preferential access to European markets that might make British trade relationships more attractive to Commonwealth partners.

The Comprehensive and Progressive Trans-Pacific Partnership (CPTPP) that Britain joined in 2023 includes several Commonwealth countries that treat Britain as one member among many rather than as Commonwealth leader. British membership in CPTPP reflects recognition that regional trade arrangements provide better economic opportunities than Commonwealth-based trade relationships.

Cultural diplomacy through Commonwealth institutions operates on minimal scales compared to American, Chinese, and regional cultural influences that shape Commonwealth societies more significantly than British cultural exports. British Council activities and cultural exchange programs compete unsuccessfully with better-funded and more relevant cultural programs offered by other countries.

The Bollywood film industry produces more cultural content for global audiences than British cultural industries, while K-pop and other Asian cultural exports attract larger audiences in Commonwealth countries than British cultural products. This cultural displacement reflects economic and technological changes that have eliminated British cultural advantages in former colonial territories.

The monarchy provides the primary institutional link between Britain and Commonwealth countries that retain constitutional monarchies, but this relationship serves ceremonial rather than practical functions while creating constitutional complications for independent nations. Republican movements in several Commonwealth countries reflect recognition that constitutional monarchy represents anachronistic imperial relationship rather than appropriate governance structure for independent nations.

Barbados became a republic in 2021, removing Queen Elizabeth II as head of state while maintaining Commonwealth membership, demonstrating that countries can abandon constitutional monarchy without affecting other international relationships. This precedent encourages republican movements in other Commonwealth countries that view constitutional monarchy as colonial anachronism rather than functional governance structure.

Constitutional arrangements that maintain British monarch as head of state in Commonwealth countries create confusion about sovereignty and democratic legitimacy while providing no practical benefits to either Britain or Commonwealth countries. These arrangements survive through inertia rather than functional value, while creating complications for international law and diplomatic protocol.

The Governor-General system that represents royal authority in Commonwealth realms operates through appointed representatives who exercise ceremonial functions while real governmental power rests with elected officials. This constitutional complexity serves no practical purpose while maintaining symbolic subordination to British monarchy that conflicts with principles of democratic sovereignty.

Legal systems based on British common law provide some continuing connection between Britain and former colonies, but these legal traditions have evolved independently in Commonwealth countries rather than maintaining dependence on British legal development. British legal expertise competes with local legal development and influences from other legal systems, while Commonwealth countries adapt their legal systems to local needs rather than British precedents.

The Judicial Committee of the Privy Council continues to serve as final court of appeal for several Commonwealth countries, but this arrangement reflects historical accident rather than legal necessity, while these countries increasingly establish their own supreme courts rather than maintaining appeals to British judicial authority. This transition to legal independence eliminates another vestige of imperial relationship.

The language advantage that English provides in international communication owes more to American economic and cultural dominance than to British imperial history, while Commonwealth countries develop independent varieties of English that diverge from British usage. British attempts to maintain language standardization through cultural institutions face competition from American cultural influences and local language development.

Indian English, Australian English, and other Commonwealth varieties have developed their own literary traditions, media industries, and cultural expressions that operate independently of British cultural influence. These linguistic developments reflect cultural independence rather than continued dependence on British cultural authority.

Educational influence through British university traditions operates in Commonwealth countries that have developed independent educational systems often superior to contemporary British education. Commonwealth students increasingly choose non-British universities for higher education, while British universities recruit Commonwealth students as fee-paying customers rather than providing educational assistance for development purposes.

The decline in Commonwealth student enrolment at British universities reflects both the improved quality of domestic and regional educational opportunities in Commonwealth countries and the deteriorating value proposition of British higher education. Brexit immigration restrictions and reduced post-graduation employment opportunities make British education less attractive to international students who can access similar or better educational opportunities elsewhere.

Until Britain acknowledges that imperial nostalgia prevents realistic assessment of contemporary international position and opportunities, British foreign policy will continue to waste resources on symbolic gestures rather than developing effective relationships with countries that could provide genuine partnership benefits. The choice facing Britain is between continued imperial mythology that serves psychological needs while achieving no practical results, and realistic foreign policy based on Britain's actual capabilities and genuine international opportunities.

The phantom empire exists only in British imagination while imposing real costs on British resources and international relationships, preventing the development of foreign policy appropriate to Britain's diminished but still significant international position. Imperial nostalgia serves domestic political needs while undermining Britain's capacity for effective international engagement based on realistic assessment of contemporary global relationships.

The ongoing conflicts in Kashmir and Nigeria demonstrate that imperial legacies continue to generate human suffering and regional instability decades after decolonization, while Britain avoids acknowledging responsibility for conflicts its colonial policies created. These cases illustrate how imperial boundary-drawing and administrative decisions created artificial states and territorial disputes that continue to destabilize entire regions while British policy-makers celebrate imperial history rather than confronting its ongoing consequences.

The transformation of imperial relationships into commercial and cultural exchanges could provide foundation for genuine partnerships based on mutual benefit rather than historical domination, but this transformation requires abandoning imperial nostalgia that prevents honest acknowledgment of colonial damage and contemporary equality between Britain and former colonial territories. Until British foreign policy operates through realistic assessment of contemporary relationships rather than imperial mythology, the phantom empire will continue to distort British international engagement while providing no practical benefits to anyone involved.

# The "Royal" Mail Scandal: When Institutions Fail

The name alone is laughable now. Still trading on that royal connection while delivering service that would embarrass a village post office from 1950. Royal Mail represents the perfect metaphor for British institutional decline: a centuries-old service that once connected an empire now struggles to deliver letters across town while maintaining the ceremonial trappings of its imperial past. The "Royal" designation has become a cruel joke, suggesting excellence and reliability while delivering incompetence and failure on an industrial scale.

The statistical evidence of Royal Mail's decline reveals a service in terminal collapse despite retaining the prestige of royal association. Stamp prices have increased by over 400% since privatization in 2013, while service quality has deteriorated across every measurable metric. First-class stamps that once guaranteed next-day delivery now cost £1.35 while taking 3-4 days to reach their destinations, transforming premium postal service into expensive disappointment. The price increases fund shareholder dividends and executive bonuses rather than service improvements, demonstrating how privatization serves financial extraction rather than public service.

"First class" mail has become a marketing fiction that bears no relationship to actual delivery performance. The commitment to next-day delivery that defined first-class service for generations has been quietly abandoned while prices continue to rise, creating the perverse situation where customers pay premium prices for service that fails to meet basic expectations. This bait-and-switch pricing strategy exemplifies how privatized public services exploit consumer trust while degrading service quality.

Saturday deliveries have been axed in many areas despite customer complaints and business needs, reducing postal service to a four-day-per-week operation that ignores modern commercial requirements. Collection times have been slashed from multiple daily collections to single pickups, often occurring before most businesses complete their daily correspondence. Post offices have closed in thousands of communities, forcing residents to travel miles for basic postal services that were once available locally.

The contrast with modern delivery services reveals the artificial nature of Royal Mail's service failures. Amazon delivers same-day and next-day packages across major British cities using the same road infrastructure that Royal Mail claims makes timely delivery impossible. Chinese sellers on eBay routinely deliver packages from Shenzhen to British customers faster than Royal Mail moves letters across town, demonstrating that efficient international logistics can outperform domestic postal service managed by supposedly expert British institutions.

This performance gap exposes the deliberate nature of Royal Mail's service degradation. The infrastructure, technology, and logistics expertise exist to provide efficient postal services, but privatization incentives reward cost-cutting over service quality while regulatory oversight fails to enforce service standards that would protect consumer interests. Royal Mail operates as profit-extraction mechanism disguised as public service.

The privatization process itself represents a masterclass in asset-stripping disguised as economic modernization. Royal Mail was sold to City investors at a fraction of its actual value, transferring public assets built over centuries to private hands for immediate profit-taking rather than long-term service improvement. The undervaluation was so egregious that shares increased by 38% on the first day of trading, representing an immediate transfer of billions of pounds from public to private ownership.

The workforce has been casualized through zero-hours contracts and reduced benefits while working conditions have deteriorated through speed-up measures and surveillance systems that treat postal workers as potential criminals rather than public servants. Union-busting tactics and management hostility have replaced the cooperative relationships that once characterized postal service employment, creating adversarial workplace relationships that inevitably affect service quality.

The postal network has been asset-stripped through property sales and facility closures that prioritize short-term revenue generation over long-term service capacity. Historic post office buildings in prime locations have been sold to property developers while postal services relocate to inferior premises or close entirely. This asset-stripping provides immediate returns to shareholders while permanently degrading postal infrastructure.

Classic British privatization playbook: take public infrastructure built over centuries, sell it for pennies to City friends, then act surprised when it stops working. The regulatory framework that supposedly protects consumer interests has proven toothless in preventing service degradation while providing cover for continued price increases and service cuts. Ofcom, the postal regulator, operates as a captured agency that prioritizes industry interests over consumer protection.

And they still slap "Royal" on everything like it means quality instead of dysfunction. The royal designation has become false advertising that exploits consumer trust while delivering service that contradicts every expectation that royal association might create. The monarchy's association with this failing service damages royal reputation while providing no protection for consumers who expect royal standards but receive corporate indifference.

But the Horizon scandal represents the perfect encapsulation of everything wrong with British institutional behaviour, combining technological incompetence, corporate dishonesty, judicial blindness, and governmental indifference to destroy hundreds of innocent lives while protecting the reputations of institutions that prioritized their own interests over truth and justice. The scandal reveals how British establishments operate when challenged: they close ranks, destroy critics, and maintain lies for decades rather than acknowledge error and accept accountability.

The Horizon computer system scandal is the killer example - hundreds of innocent postmasters prosecuted, lives destroyed, suicides, all to cover up their IT contractor's failures. The establishment knew and kept quiet for years. Classic British institutional behaviour - protect the system, sacrifice the people. Between 1999 and 2015, the Post Office prosecuted over 730 sub-postmasters for theft, fraud, and false accounting based entirely on evidence from a computer system that the Post Office knew was unreliable. These prosecutions destroyed lives, families, and communities while enriching lawyers, consultants, and executives who participated in a cover-up that continued for over two decades.

The scale of institutional failure revealed by the Horizon scandal staggers belief. These prosecutions destroyed lives, families, and communities while enriching lawyers, consultants, and executives who participated in a cover-up that continued for over two decades. The scandal represents the largest miscarriage of justice in British legal history, demonstrating how British institutions operate when their interests conflict with truth and justice.

The Horizon computer system, developed by Fujitsu, contained fundamental flaws that created phantom transactions, duplicated entries, and generated accounting discrepancies that made sub-postmasters' accounts appear to show missing money. The Post Office knew about these technical problems from the system's inception but chose to prosecute sub-postmasters rather than acknowledge software failures that would have undermined confidence in postal services and cost millions of pounds to rectify.

Internal Post Office documents revealed during litigation show that senior executives, legal advisors, and IT specialists knew that Horizon created false accounting data but deliberately concealed this information from defence lawyers, judges, and government ministers. This concealment constituted criminal conspiracy to pervert the course of justice, yet none of the Post Office officials responsible for orchestrating this cover-up have faced prosecution for their crimes.

The human cost of this institutional conspiracy cannot be measured in purely financial terms, though the economic damage inflicted on innocent families was catastrophic. Sub-postmasters faced demands to repay tens of thousands of pounds in allegedly missing money, forcing them to sell homes, exhaust savings, and borrow against personal assets to cover losses that existed only in faulty computer records. Many lost their livelihoods, their homes, and their reputations while suffering prosecution for crimes they did not commit.

## The Human Wreckage: Real Lives Destroyed

The individual stories of Horizon victims reveal the personal catastrophe that institutional failure inflicted on ordinary people who trusted British justice to protect them from false accusations. These stories demonstrate how institutional power can destroy individual lives while avoiding accountability for the suffering it creates.

Jo Hamilton, a sub-postmistress from Hampshire, discovered discrepancies in her accounts that she could not explain despite meticulous record-keeping and years of experience managing postal services. When Horizon showed £36,000 missing from her accounts, Hamilton initially assumed she had made errors and used her own money to cover the discrepancy. The Post Office investigation concluded that she must have stolen the money, leading to criminal prosecution despite Hamilton's clean record and obvious distress about the allegations.

Hamilton pleaded guilty to false accounting in 2008 to avoid prison sentence, accepting criminal conviction rather than fighting charges that would have resulted in imprisonment and left her children without support. This guilty plea destroyed her reputation in the community where she had worked for decades, forcing her family to relocate while she struggled with depression and anxiety caused by criminal conviction for crimes she had not committed.

The psychological impact on Hamilton included persistent anxiety, difficulty sleeping, and constant worry about her children's futures in light of her criminal record. She developed medical problems related to stress while struggling to find employment that would accept workers with criminal convictions for financial offenses. The conviction affected her entire family, with her children facing questions at school about their mother's criminal record.

Hamilton's marriage suffered under the strain of financial pressure and community suspicion, while extended family relationships became strained due to doubts about her innocence. The social isolation that followed criminal conviction compounded the financial hardship, creating comprehensive life disruption that extended far beyond the immediate legal consequences of false prosecution.

Seema Misra, a sub-postmistress from Surrey, faced prosecution while pregnant with her second child, enduring trial and sentencing while coping with pregnancy complications caused by stress from false accusations. Misra was sentenced to 15 months' imprisonment in 2010, serving her sentence in Bronzefield women's prison while her infant son was cared for by family members.

The separation from her young children caused lasting psychological trauma for both Misra and her family, while the conviction destroyed her husband's business and forced the family into debt. Prison medical records show that Misra suffered complications during her pregnancy that doctors attributed to stress from prosecution, while her older child developed behavioural problems related to his mother's absence.

After release from prison, Misra struggled to rebuild relationships with her children while dealing with post-traumatic stress from imprisonment and ongoing financial pressure from legal costs. The family home was remortgaged to pay legal expenses, while Misra's criminal record prevented employment in positions requiring financial responsibility. The conviction affected her immigration status, creating additional legal complications that required expensive legal representation.

The impact on Misra's extended family included ostracism from community members who believed the criminal conviction proved guilt, while cultural pressures within the South Asian community created additional shame and isolation. Family relationships became strained as relatives struggled to understand how Misra could have been convicted if she was innocent, creating doubt and suspicion that persisted even after the conviction was overturned.

Alan Bates, the sub-postmaster who led the campaign for justice, endured decades of financial pressure while fighting to expose the Horizon scandal. Bates faced legal costs exceeding £100,000 while pursuing litigation against the Post Office, forcing him to remortgage his home and exhaust retirement savings to fund legal action that the justice system should have provided without cost to victims.

The stress of leading the campaign while managing his own case caused health problems including high blood pressure and cardiac issues that required medical treatment. Bates described periods of severe depression when the legal process seemed hopeless and the Post Office appeared likely to escape accountability for its actions. The psychological burden of representing hundreds of other victims created additional pressure beyond his personal legal concerns.

Bates's marriage endured significant strain due to financial pressure and the emotional demands of fighting institutional injustice, while his children's educational and career opportunities were affected by family financial constraints caused by legal costs.

The campaign consumed years of his life that could have been devoted to family and personal interests, creating opportunity costs that cannot be recovered even with successful legal resolution.

## The Ultimate Tragedy: Martin Griffiths and the Suicide of Innocence

The most heartbreaking consequence of the Horizon scandal is the suicide of Martin Griffiths, a sub-postmaster whose death demonstrates how institutional failure can literally kill innocent people who become trapped in systems designed to protect institutions rather than individuals.

Martin Griffiths managed a post office in Ellesmere Port, Cheshire, where he served the local community for years without incident until Horizon began showing discrepancies in his accounts. Like hundreds of other sub-postmasters, Griffiths could not explain missing money that existed only in computer records, but the Post Office investigation assumed guilt rather than investigating technical problems that might explain the discrepancies.

The Post Office suspended Griffiths from his position and began criminal investigation that treated him as a thief rather than a victim of technical failures. The suspension meant immediate loss of income for Griffiths and his family, while the criminal investigation created stress that affected his physical and mental health. Friends and family described Griffiths as becoming increasingly withdrawn and depressed as the investigation proceeded.

Griffiths faced the impossible choice that confronted all Horizon victims: plead guilty to crimes he had not committed or fight charges that could result in imprisonment and complete financial ruin. The Post Office presented its computer evidence as infallible while concealing known technical problems that created false accounting data. Defence lawyers could not challenge computer evidence without access to technical information that the Post Office refused to provide.

The psychological pressure of facing criminal charges for theft while knowing his innocence created unbearable stress for Griffiths, who had built his identity around honesty and community service. The prospect of imprisonment and permanent criminal conviction for financial crimes seemed to offer no possibility of redemption or restoration of reputation, even if he eventually proved his innocence.

On September 23, 2013, Martin Griffiths took his own life, leaving behind a wife and children who lost not only their husband and father but also their primary income and their home. His suicide note expressed despair about the criminal charges and fear that his family would suffer permanent shame from his conviction for crimes he had not committed.

The Post Office response to Griffiths's suicide demonstrated institutional callousness that prioritized reputation management over human decency. Rather than investigating whether false prosecution had contributed to his death, the Post Office continued pursuing other Horizon cases while maintaining that its computer system was reliable and its prosecutions were justified.

Griffiths's family faced additional trauma after his death, struggling with grief while dealing with financial pressure from lost income and legal costs. The suicide created lasting psychological damage for his children, who lost their father while struggling to understand how innocent people could be driven to suicide by false accusations from trusted institutions.

The community impact of Griffiths's death extended beyond his immediate family to other sub-postmasters who recognized that institutional pressure could destroy lives regardless of innocence or guilt.

His suicide demonstrated that the Post Office was prepared to pursue prosecutions even when the human cost became fatal, creating fear among other Horizon victims who worried that they might face similar desperation.

The investigation into Griffiths's death failed to examine whether Post Office actions had contributed to his suicide, while coronial proceedings focused on individual mental health rather than institutional responsibility for creating the circumstances that led to his despair. This investigative failure allowed the Post Office to avoid accountability for the human consequences of its prosecutorial practices.

Julian Wilson, another sub-postmaster from London, also took his own life in 2005 after facing prosecution for alleged theft that existed only in Horizon computer records. Wilson had served his community for over a decade when the computer system began showing discrepancies that he could not explain. The Post Office treated these discrepancies as evidence of theft rather than investigating technical problems that might explain the missing money.

Wilson's death occurred early in the Horizon scandal, before the scale of technical problems became apparent to victims and their families. His suicide was treated as individual tragedy rather than institutional failure, allowing the Post Office to continue prosecutions while avoiding scrutiny about whether its practices contributed to sub-postmaster deaths.

The families of both Griffiths and Wilson have struggled for justice while dealing with grief compounded by knowledge that their loved ones died defending their innocence against false accusations. These families represent the ultimate victims of institutional failure that literally killed innocent people while protecting the reputations of organizations that prioritized their interests over human life.

## Institutional Conspiracy and Cover-Up

The Horizon scandal reveals how British institutions operate when their interests conflict with truth and justice. Rather than acknowledging technical problems and compensating victims, the Post Office, Fujitsu, government ministers, and legal authorities conspired to maintain false narratives that protected institutional reputations while destroying innocent lives.

Senior Post Office executives including Paula Vennells, who later received a CBE for services to the Post Office, knew that Horizon contained technical flaws that created false accounting data but authorized continued prosecutions based on unreliable computer evidence. Internal emails revealed during litigation show that Vennells and other executives discussed the reputational risks of acknowledging technical problems while continuing to authorize prosecutions they knew were based on false evidence.

The legal department at the Post Office, led by solicitors who understood that Horizon evidence was unreliable, developed prosecution strategies that concealed technical problems from defence lawyers and judges. These lawyers drafted court documents that presented computer evidence as infallible while possessing internal reports documenting system failures that created false accounting data.

Fujitsu engineers who developed and maintained Horizon knew that the system contained bugs that created phantom transactions and accounting discrepancies but failed to alert prosecutors or defence lawyers about technical problems that undermined the reliability of computer evidence. The company's commercial interests in maintaining lucrative Post Office contracts took precedence over honesty about technical failures that affected criminal prosecutions.

Government ministers responsible for postal services received briefings about Horizon problems but chose to support Post Office management rather than investigating whether innocent people were being prosecuted based on false computer evidence. This ministerial support continued even after MPs raised concerns about the unusually high number of prosecutions involving sub-postmasters and the consistent pattern of accounting discrepancies.

The Criminal Cases Review Commission, which investigates potential miscarriages of justice, initially rejected applications from Horizon victims despite evidence suggesting systematic problems with Post Office prosecutions. The Commission's failure to investigate these cases promptly allowed the scandal to continue for years while additional innocent people faced prosecution based on known unreliable evidence.

Crown Prosecution Service lawyers who handled Horizon cases failed to scrutinize Post Office evidence adequately, accepting computer data as reliable without investigating technical problems that might affect its accuracy. This prosecutorial failure reflected systemic problems with how British courts handle technical evidence in criminal cases.

Judges who presided over Horizon trials accepted Post Office assertions about computer reliability without requiring technical proof that the systems produced accurate data. The judicial failure to scrutinize technical evidence reflected assumptions about institutional credibility that proved catastrophically wrong in cases where institutions actively concealed evidence that undermined their positions.

## The Cover-Up Continues

Even after the scale of the Horizon scandal became apparent, British institutions continued to prioritize reputation management over justice for victims. The Post Office fought compensation claims and appeals while senior executives received honours and bonuses for maintaining postal services during the period when they were knowingly prosecuting innocent people.

Paula Vennells received a CBE in 2019 for services to the Post Office, demonstrating how the honours system rewards institutional loyalty rather than honesty or justice. Vennells and other senior executives received performance bonuses while Horizon victims struggled with bankruptcy and criminal records, illustrating the different standards applied to institutional insiders and ordinary citizens.

The government response to the scandal prioritized limiting compensation costs rather than ensuring justice for victims, with ministers arguing that full compensation would create unsustainable financial liability for public funds. This cost-focused approach ignored the fact that government inaction had allowed the scandal to continue for decades while innocent people suffered prosecution and imprisonment.

Legal processes for overturning wrongful convictions proceeded slowly due to Post Office resistance and insufficient resources allocated to reviewing cases, forcing victims to wait years for exoneration while dealing with ongoing consequences of criminal convictions. The adversarial approach taken by Post Office lawyers created additional trauma for victims who faced aggressive cross-examination about their honesty and competence.

Fujitsu faced minimal accountability for its role in creating and concealing technical problems that led to wrongful prosecutions, with the company continuing to receive government contracts despite its documented dishonesty about system reliability. The failure to hold Fujitsu accountable sent a clear message that technical companies could conceal critical flaws in systems used for criminal prosecutions without facing serious consequences.

The public inquiry into the scandal, while necessary, proceeded slowly while victims aged and died, with some Horizon victims passing away before receiving exoneration or compensation for the wrongful prosecutions they endured. The delayed inquiry response reflected institutional priorities that treated the scandal as a manageable crisis rather than a fundamental failure requiring urgent redress.

The Broader Pattern of Institutional Failure

The Horizon scandal represents a microcosm of broader patterns in British institutional behaviour that prioritize organizational reputation over individual justice. These patterns appear consistently across different institutions and time periods, suggesting systematic problems with how British establishments respond to evidence of institutional failure.

The banking scandals that preceded the 2008 financial crisis revealed similar patterns of institutional dishonesty and regulatory capture, with financial institutions concealing risks while regulators failed to investigate obvious warning signs. The human cost of banking failures affected millions of people through job losses, home repossessions, and pension fund losses, yet senior bankers faced minimal accountability for their roles in creating systemic risks.

The contaminated blood scandal that affected over 5,000 NHS patients revealed decades of institutional cover-up similar to the Horizon scandal, with health authorities concealing knowledge about infection risks while continuing practices they knew were dangerous. Victims of contaminated blood products faced years of denial and legal obstruction before receiving acknowledgment of institutional responsibility.

The Hillsborough disaster investigation revealed police and media institutions conspiring to blame victims rather than acknowledging operational failures that caused deaths. The institutional response involved falsifying evidence, manipulating media coverage, and obstructing investigations for decades before truth emerged through persistent campaigning by victims' families.

The Grenfell Tower fire exposed similar patterns of institutional failure and subsequent cover-up, with building authorities, construction companies, and government departments prioritizing cost reduction over fire safety while concealing known risks that led to preventable deaths. The post-fire response has involved legal obstruction and delay tactics that prevent accountability while victims' families struggle for justice

## The International Dimension

The Horizon scandal has damaged Britain's international reputation for judicial integrity and technological competence, with foreign observers expressing amazement that British institutions could maintain such a systematic cover-up for over two decades. International legal experts have cited the scandal as evidence of fundamental problems with British approaches to criminal justice and institutional accountability.

The European Court of Human Rights has received applications from Horizon victims claiming that British justice failed to provide fair trials, while international media coverage has portrayed the scandal as evidence of British institutional decay. These international responses undermine British soft power and diplomatic influence while reinforcing perceptions of British decline.

Technology companies operating internationally have cited the Horizon scandal as evidence that technical evidence in criminal cases requires independent verification rather than institutional assurances about system reliability. The scandal has influenced international best practices for handling computer evidence in criminal prosecutions, with foreign jurisdictions implementing safeguards that Britain lacks.

The failure to hold Fujitsu accountable for its role in the scandal has implications for international technology contracts, with foreign governments potentially viewing British regulatory oversight as inadequate for ensuring corporate honesty about system reliability. This reputational damage affects British technology exports and international competitiveness in sectors requiring high trust and reliability.

## The Compensation Farce

The compensation process for Horizon victims has demonstrated continued institutional priorities that Favor cost control over victim welfare, with complex procedures and inadequate payments that fail to address the comprehensive damage caused by wrongful prosecutions. The compensation scheme requires victims to prove financial losses with precision while ignoring psychological damage and opportunity costs that cannot be calculated precisely.

Maximum compensation payments of £600,000 per victim represent inadequate recognition of comprehensive life damage caused by wrongful prosecution, imprisonment, and decades of living with criminal convictions. Many victims have received far less than maximum payments due to difficulties proving losses and Post Office challenges to compensation claims.

The requirement for victims to accept compensation offers without legal recourse prevents adequate compensation for the most severely affected victims, while creating pressure to accept inadequate payments rather than pursuing full justice through lengthy legal processes. This approach protects public finances while failing to provide proportionate redress for institutional failures.

Legal costs for pursuing compensation often consume substantial portions of compensation awards, with victims forced to pay expensive lawyers to navigate complex procedures designed to minimize compensation payments. The adversarial compensation process creates additional trauma while enriching legal professionals rather than adequately compensating victims.

The exclusion of family members from compensation eligibility ignores the reality that wrongful prosecutions affect entire families through financial pressure, social stigma, and psychological trauma. Spouses and children of Horizon victims suffered consequences of institutional failure without access to compensation for their losses.

## The Technological Legacy

The Horizon scandal has revealed fundamental problems with how British institutions handle technology evidence in criminal cases, with courts accepting corporate assurances about system reliability without requiring independent technical verification. These problems affect other criminal cases involving computer evidence, suggesting that the Horizon scandal may represent only the most visible example of systematic problems with technology evidence.

The Post Office Horizon system continues to operate with modifications but without fundamental redesign to address the technical problems that created false accounting data. This continuation suggests that institutional learning from the scandal has been limited, with technical fixes preferred over comprehensive system replacement that would acknowledge the scale of original failures.

Other government computer systems face similar reliability questions without adequate oversight or independent verification, creating potential for future scandals involving false evidence from unreliable technical systems. The failure to implement comprehensive reforms following the Horizon scandal suggests that similar problems could affect other technology-dependent criminal proceedings.

The legal precedents established by Horizon prosecutions continue to influence how courts handle computer evidence, with judges potentially accepting technical evidence without adequate scrutiny due to assumptions about institutional credibility that the scandal has thoroughly undermined. This legacy effect could affect future criminal cases involving technical evidence.

## The Continuing Scandal

The Horizon scandal continues to unfold as additional evidence emerges about the extent of institutional knowledge about system failures and the deliberate concealment of information that could have prevented wrongful prosecutions. New documents released during ongoing inquiries reveal broader institutional conspiracy than previously acknowledged, suggesting that the full scale of the scandal remains unknown.

Additional Horizon victims continue to come forward as publicity about the scandal encourages people who accepted criminal convictions to seek exoneration, suggesting that the 730 prosecutions represent only the documented cases rather than the complete universe of wrongful convictions. Many victims may have died or chosen not to pursue exoneration due to trauma from their original prosecutions.

The technological problems that caused the original scandal may have affected additional criminal cases beyond Post Office prosecutions, with police investigations and other government proceedings potentially relying on similar unreliable computer evidence. The systemic nature of problems with technology evidence suggests that the Horizon scandal may represent only the most visible example of broader institutional failures.

International investigations into Fujitsu's role in other government technology contracts may reveal similar patterns of concealing technical problems while maintaining contracts based on assurances about system reliability. The company's approach to the Horizon contract suggests systematic corporate practices that prioritize commercial interests over honesty about technical capabilities.

The combination of Royal Mail's general service decline with the specific criminality of the Horizon scandal creates a perfect storm of institutional failure that destroys public trust while enriching private interests. The Royal designation has become a mark of shame rather than quality, while the postal service that once connected an empire now struggles to connect neighbouring streets.

The privatization model that produced these failures represents the broader pattern of British institutional decline: public assets sold cheap to private interests, services degraded for profit extraction, and accountability eliminated through regulatory capture. The Royal Mail scandal encapsulates everything wrong with how Britain manages its institutions, prioritizing short-term private gain over long-term public service while maintaining ceremonial pretences that mock the reality of systematic failure.

The Horizon scandal represents the perfect encapsulation of British institutional failure: technological incompetence disguised as innovation, corporate dishonesty protected by regulatory capture, judicial blindness to obvious injustice, and political indifference to human suffering caused by institutional prioritization of reputation over truth. The scandal continues because British institutions remain fundamentally unchanged despite overwhelming evidence of systematic failure that destroyed hundreds of innocent lives while enriching the officials responsible for orchestrating decades of cover-up.

Until British institutions learn to prioritize truth and justice over reputation management and cost control, similar scandals will continue to destroy innocent lives while protecting the officials whose decisions create institutional failures. The Horizon scandal provides the template for how British establishments respond to evidence of failure: deny, delay, and destroy critics while maintaining systems that serve institutional interests rather than public welfare. This template will persist until external pressure forces institutional change that British establishments will never initiate voluntarily.

The "Royal" Mail scandal represents the death of any legitimate claim to British institutional integrity, revealing a system where innocence provides no protection against institutional power and where justice serves organizational reputation rather than individual rights. The phantom empire's final colony is the British people themselves, subject to institutions that operate with imperial arrogance while providing colonial standards of justice and accountability.

The name "Royal Mail" has become false advertising on an epic scale, a designation that promises excellence while delivering failure, suggests reliability while providing chaos, and claims royal standards while achieving systematic criminality. The royal connection that once meant quality assurance now serves as warning about institutional corruption disguised as traditional authority. Until Britain learns to judge institutions by their performance rather than their titles, the "Royal" designation will continue to mark failure rather than excellence, serving private interests rather than public welfare while destroying the lives of innocent people who trusted British justice to protect them from institutional criminality.

# A Conclusion

Thank you for purchasing "Keep Calm And Listen" and, more importantly, for having the courage to read it through to the end. I know this has not been an easy journey. Over these fifteen chapters, I have systematically dismantled cherished beliefs about British exceptionalism, confronted comfortable myths with uncomfortable truths, and presented evidence that many would prefer to ignore. The fact that you have stayed with me through this unflinching examination of British decline suggests you understand that honest diagnosis, however painful, is the necessary first step toward genuine recovery.

My hope is that this book has fundamentally changed how you see the country around you, that you can no longer watch politicians invoke the "special relationship" without remembering its one-sided reality, or listen to NHS worship without thinking of preventable deaths, or hear weather complaints without recognizing them as sophisticated avoidance of serious conversation. If I have succeeded, you now possess a kind of double vision: the ability to see both the Britain that exists in national mythology and the Britain that actually functions day to day. This cognitive dissonance should be uncomfortable. It should make you angry. That anger is not a weakness, it is the beginning of the energy needed for change.

The conversations this book generates matter more than the book itself. Every dinner party discussion about housing speculation, every pub argument about queue culture, every social media debate about imperial nostalgia represents a small victory against the conspiracy of silence that protects institutional failure from public scrutiny. Change begins when enough people stop accepting convenient fictions and start demanding inconvenient truths. Britain's problems are not mysteries requiring expert solutions, they are well-documented failures requiring political will to address. But political will emerges only when public opinion shifts, and public opinion shifts only when comfortable delusions become socially unacceptable.

Sitting still and hoping for improvement guarantees continued decline dressed up as managed transition. But pointing out flaws, having difficult conversations, and ultimately taking action can still redirect this country's trajectory toward something resembling its potential rather than its current performance. Britain's advantages, its educated population, democratic traditions, global connections, and cultural influence, remain real despite decades of institutional mismanagement. The question is whether enough people will demand that these advantages be used intelligently rather than squandered nostalgically. The future is not predetermined. It remains, as always, a choice. The only question is whether Britain will choose honestly or continue choosing mythology. Thank you for choosing to look into the mirror. Now help others do the same.

Printed in Dunstable, United Kingdom